How To Get More Clients

Mike Considine

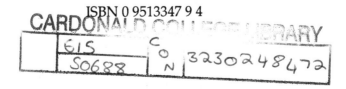

Brainwave
Address correspondence to:
BCM Brainwave
London WC1N 3XX
England
Phone: 0181-677 8000   Fax: 0181-677 4035
Email: brain@mail.zynet.co.uk

ISBN 0 9513347 9 4

About the Author

Since he was twenty three years old Mike Considine has had an intense interest in therapy. He has had experience in many different therapies such as gestalt, bio-energetics, Rolfing, Alexander technique, transactional analysis, massage, acupuncture, shiatsu, osteopathy, nlp and many others. He subequently trained in gestalt therapy and practiced for several years subsequently, before becoming involved in publishing and marketing in the holistic field.

He holds a masters degree in psychology from Antioch University (London), where he conducted research into the phenomena of transference in twenty small psychotherapy groups. He further undertook research for six years into transference for a doctorate in psychology at Sussex University.

He has written and compiled *Holistic London, Survivor's London, The Whole Person Catalogue, The Holistic Marketing Directory*, and *The Gift Marketing Directory*.

He presently runs a marketing and promotion company for people in the holistic field, is the editor and publisher of *Holistic London Guide* and organises holistic festivals in London.

Dedication

This book is dedicated to my loving wife Kate, and Sam our adorable toddler. They are both a great source of inspiration and delight to me.

Preface

This book is intended for counsellors, complementary medicine practitioners, holisitic therapists, spiritual teachers, workshops leaders, readers of tarot and astrologers. It aims to empower the practitioner with the business skills that are essential to get more clients.

If you are already a therapist and have been practising for a while, you probably realise that getting clients is a difficult and ongoing affair. More likely than not, the subject of how to get more clients was not covered in your training. You probably gave scant attention to it at the time. Fair enough. You were busy learning your chosen art, probably in the middle of changing your profession, and didn't have much time for lectures on marketing.

Finally, however, you finished your training. It was time to practice your new healing art, and you needed clients to practice. Only then did you realise that getting fee-paying clients is also an art, but one that you were not versed in. This book is intended to fill that gap - to provide you with necessary skills in marketing and public relations.

From my experience, those who survive in the therapy business are the people who have mastered the art of marketing and public relations. Either they have brought these previously learned skills to their new profession, or they take quickly and easily to marketing from the start. The practitioners that fall by the wayside are those who lack these basic business skills. These less successful therapists often blame themselves. They come to the conclusion they are poor practitioners, find a new job and eventually come out of private practice. In my experience, this is a tremendous and unnecessary waste of talent and energy.

This book covers the methods of gaining marketing and public relations skills that you can use to get more clients and establish a healthy, thriving business. It will empower you with the skills you need to build and maintain a successful practice.

Contents

# Introduction

Business & Healing: Conflicting Ideals?

Some people think that healing and business have conflicting ideals: business is a hard-hearted and demanding practice, healing is a gentle and caring way of life. These are myths. One of the many definitions of the word business is 'the activity which affords one his livelihood'. If you are a healer, you are in the business of healing and you are hoping to earn your livelihood in this manner.

Of course, the practice of the healing arts and the art of making money are two quite different activities. You have to do both. You can't be a therapist without earning money, and you don't want to earn your money any other way.

Many people think that if they do what they enjoy, the money will flow in. This is only partially true. If you do what you enjoy and you exercise some discipline with it, then the money will flow in.

As a therapist, you will have a lot of 'non therapy' work that is just as time-consuming (and potentially tedious) as the work at any other job. You will have to keep your accounts in meticulous order, draw up budgets, save all your receipts, go through the agony of filing your VAT return and your taxes. You will want to keep records of all your clients past and present, deal with complaints, answer enquiries, write business letters. You will need to plan all of your activities six months in advance, promote yourself *and* network.

Enjoyment & Vision is the Plan

The key to a fulfilling and successful life is that you enjoy what you do. Not surprisingly, this is also the key to being a successful practitioner.

If you enjoy what you do, you will have the energy and positive attitude you need to cope with the obstacles you face. If you aren't enjoying yourself or if you are not doing what you really want to be doing, everything will be a struggle.

Of course, there are times when we feel there is no alternative than taking a job we actively dislike because we need the money. We all need to earn a living.

However, if you find you are giving too much of your energy to things that you don't enjoy or care about, it's time to rethink your life. It can take a lot of courage to let go of financial security, even if you hate your job! To prepare yourself and make changing your career a lot easier, you will have to lay down some solid financial foundations. This will enable you to finally do what you really want and earn a living at the same time.

Your vision

You trained in your discipline because you had a vision. You had an idea, a plan, a direction to follow in your life. You were attracted to your practice for some reason.

Everyone's motives are different. Some people become therapists because they themselves received therapy that worked for them; some because they enjoy working with people and helping others; some because they want to make positive contributions to their community.

Similarly, everyone is going in a different direction with their practice. Some people want to ultimately run their own centre, with a network of other therapists around them; some people want to spend as much time with their family as they can, and see therapy as being the perfect profession for this and some want to ultimately teach their therapy to others.

Maybe all you know is that you enjoy what you are doing, and that is enough, as long as your inspiration and your motivation does not dry up. Defining your vision and your direction are both ways of preventing this and ways of keeping up the momentum of moving forward and improving.

Your needs

Fine, you have a vision, you have a direction, you are inspired, but you also have needs that inspiration alone is not going meet.

First of all, you need to earn a living. You need money, therefore you need paying clients. There are a number of ways to go about attracting more clients which will be discussed further later on in the book, but the most important method of getting clients is possessing enthusiasm and enjoying yourself. If you are happy in what you are doing, your work will reflect it; if your work reflects your happiness, you will attract people to your business; if you attract people to your business, you will be successful; if you are successful, you will be happy. And so it goes.

Of course, in order to be enthusiastic and happy, you have personal and emotional needs that must be met. What can you do in your life to meet these needs? Do you have enough spare time to nurture your relationships? Would you like more? Are you healthy? What do you need to do to improve your health? Do you want to travel, study, work abroad?

When you know what you want, and what you need to achieve it, you can work towards creating your ideal lifestyle, a lifestyle that you have chosen and that suits your needs. The progress may be slow but if you are happy you won't mind.

Goals

Set yourself some goals. These could be a six -month plan or a twelve month plan. Imagine where you see yourself in six month's time or in a year's time. How do you imagine yourself in five year's time? Try to imagine what you want to be doing in five years. Will you be a single practitioner or working with others. How much time do you want to spend working? Will you form a collective? These long-term goals can be incorporated into your financial plan.

Becoming a Success

Working as an independent therapist involves doing a variety of different jobs. You will need to become an accountant, marketing expert, publicist, networker, copywriter, receptionist, PR manager and so on. There is a lot to learn if you are setting out to become a therapist on your own. You will find yourself doing things that you never imagined. Being a practitioner will be only part of your job.

Even if you are planning to work at a centre to avoid all these extracurricular tasks, you will have to become a private detective in order to find the centre which suits you best. Once you've decided on one, you still have to do your own advertising, bookkeeping, stock taking, etc. Running a successful business will require you to devote a lot of time to every aspect of your business. For example, if you spend enough time on market research, your advertising and promotional efforts will be successful. Carefully chosen copy and well thought out design will result in an attractive leaflet and effective advertising.

As a practitioner, you will spend between one third and a half of your time doing something other than seeing clients. You may only be spending ten hours a week with clients, but find yourself working an additional ten hours promoting yourself, answering enquiries, planning future events and balancing your accounts.

At some point, you may even decide that you can't or won't do all of this extracurricular work and decide to hire a part-time receptionist. Employing someone to help out can be a great way of getting some psychological support, because you will have someone who is on 'your side'. Of course, it will also free up your time and energy so that you can do the things that you enjoy.

However, you will probably find that there is no way to avoid running your practice single handed. This might not be such a huge problem. Since you are looking after every aspect of your business, you can make sure that everything is done properly, and lack of communication will never be a problem. However, it is vital that your fees reflect the time and energy it takes to do all this 'extracurricular' work.

Knowing Your Strengths

We all have natural strengths and weaknesses. Some things we are really good at, other things are a struggle. Try to be aware of your strengths and use them to help yourself and your business; be mindful of your weaknesses and you can work around them.

For example, if you are hopeless at managing your finances, make sure you get as much help with this as possible. You may be someone who is a natural leader and enjoys organising groups of people or perhaps you prefer to stay out of the limelight but are good at working with people one to one.

Your natural attributes will dictate how you go about all aspects of your business. How you go about networking, for instance, will depend on your *people skills*. If you have many contacts, you will enjoy spreading news of your business all over the city; if you are quite shy, you will prefer to take the more anonymous route of advertising in magazines and newspapers. Any peripheral work you take on as a therapist will also depend on your natural strengths - there are so many sidelines in the therapy business. If you are an effective writer, you could write a book to promote yourself and garner some critical acclaim. Maybe you are a natural teacher: set up a training course! The better you know yourself, your strengths and weaknesses, the more successful you will be.

Previous experiences

Consider what experiences you have had in the past that could be of use to you now. What skills have you learned that you could use now to promote your business?

It may seem that there is no link between what you have done in the past and what you do now, but if you look for the connection carefully, you will probably be amazed. We all have many different qualities, skills and characteristics picked up and adopted throughout life. We are all unique and you need to discover what you have learned that you can use now. To clarify things you could try to list your skills under different groups like physical/practical, intellectual/mental, emotional/intuitive.

Presenting Yourself

With regards to becoming a successful therapist, it may seem unfair and superficial to spend too much time on your personal presentation, but the truth is that the public will (initially) judge you on how you present yourself. You need to present yourself in a way that will fit in with what your clients expect.

For example, if you are doing massage 'on location' in a corporate environment, you will need a corporate image yourself. You will have to dress appropriately, look efficient and have glossy brochures. If you are doing body therapies (massage, yoga, tai chi) you should look relaxed and be able to convey this impression to your clients. The public will expect you to have benefitted personally from your practice.

Consider yourself a walking, talking advertisement for your practice. You must appear efficient, friendly, positive and knowledgeable about what you are doing. Being confident and self-possessed is a skill that some people have naturally, and some people work for years to attain.

Where To Work

Working From Home

Working from home appears to be the perfect situation. It is ideal for some people, but there are many things to consider before starting a home-based practice.

No room rental

One of the main attractions of working from home is that it saves you money. Lots of money. Since you don't have to pay room rental or travel costs, your expenses are dramatically lower. Renting a room at a centre can cost up to £8 an hour, and you have to pay regardless of whether you have a client or not.

No travelling

Travelling to work takes time and money. So working at home can be more convenient and offers greater flexibility as you don't have to fit into someone else's timetable. You are more in control of when you work. Also if a client fails to appear then you haven't wasted time travelling.

Setting up costs

If you decide to set up at home, don't forget initial setting up costs such as necessary equipment, decorating, or any alterations. You should also consider that the phone and electricity bills may increase.

Special therapy room

If you don't have a separate entrance, the next best thing is to set a room aside to use solely as a therapy room. A room on the ground floor is best because your clients won't have to climb the stairs. This could be an impossibility for disabled people.

Using a ground floor room will also help to keep the most personal rooms in the house completely out of sight and separate from the treatment room. For example, locating the therapy room as far away from the bedroom as possible will help keep your personal and private life apart. It will also promote a more professional image.

Making do

Turning the sitting room or bedroom into a massage or counselling room every evening can be exhausting, time consuming and may mean kicking out others who want to use the room too! There are clearly drawbacks in using your living quarters for business, particularly for counsellors. The *vibes* that are created during a session are difficult to ignore or forget if they are in your own living room or bedroom. This invasion of your privacy could be a stressful option for you and your family or flat mates

Professional or amateur image

The informality of working at home can be relaxing and comforting to a client, who may feel more able to be themselves in a trusting, friendly environment. Others may feel uncomfortable in what is your *personal space*. It could appear amateurish. It depends on the client: some will like it, others won't.

Peace and quiet

It is essential that you can practice in peace, without distractions. This can be difficult to achieve at home, especially if there are children about. Even the background noise of a television can be too much.

Practising at home can put a lot of pressure on the people you live with. They must make numerous allowances for your business - no noise, no using the bedroom between such and such an hour and having to avoid the front door at such and such a time! It might make more sense to rent the spare room out to a tenant and to use that extra money for a room at a centre.

Waiting room

On occasion, your client will have to wait for a treatment - we all have times when things don't quite run on schedule. Someone turns up a bit late, an hour early or the roof of your house blows off in a freak storm. Anything could happen, so you should be prepared for those times when your clients have to wait for you.

You needn't provide an entire room, but you should make sure that your client has a comfortable chair and something to read in case there is a bit of an overlap. This is probably going to further cut into your own personal space, but is something you should consider before you start inviting clients into your home.

If you can't provide a place for waiting, you will need to allow more time between appointments. Or you will have to tell people not to come early because you have no waiting room (try to put this nicely, it can come across as unfriendly).

Pets

Pets can be a problem. Not everyone loves Mui Mui as much as you do! Many people are absolutely terrified of animals and would find bumping into your favourite pet a less than relaxing experience: dogs make noise, animal hairs get everywhere (making your efforts to create a clean environment quite hopeless), many people are allergic to pets (their constant sneezing could be off-putting).

If you do have a pet, try to keep it out of the therapy room and, although it may sound cruel, make sure that it is securely shut away somewhere when a client is in the house. Who knows, maybe your pet appreciates the clients even less than they do him.

Personal security

Inviting strangers to your home can be risky and personal security is something to consider. The danger of assault by a client or someone acting as a client is real. When an unknown client comes to your house, you should ensure that someone else is there, and that they are keeping an eye out for you. Leaving a radio on in another room can also be a deterrent.

Many female therapists choose to work with other women only. This can reduce the risks of personal assault and diminish feelings of vulnerability.

Although the actual risk is very minimal, steps should be taken if you are feeling anxious. It is difficult to give your undivided attention to a client when you are feeling at risk.

Nasty phone calls

Another small risk is that you will receive nuisance phone calls which are upsetting and stressful to deal with. After all, you are making your telephone number widely known. Using an answering machine to screen your calls can help.

Installing a business line, although an expense, will also protect your family from such calls and they won't have to take endless messages for you, unless you are lucky enough to have a partner or flatmate who enjoys acting as a receptionist. A separate line also prevents your home from feeling like a 24 hour office in which you are constantly available.

Risk of theft

It is worth considering protecting your property from theft. Keep valuables out of sight or locked away, and avoid leaving people alone in rooms where there is something worth pinching or a phone to misuse. Keep in mind that it is possible to get over cautious or paranoid about these risks. Just use common sense, a bit of intuition and be aware of the dangers.

Lack of support and feedback from other therapists

Working at home can be a lonely business compared to working at a health centre where there are other therapists for support and feedback.

Being part of a network of therapists is important for your business. You will make useful contacts and avoid missing out on any big events.

Legal problems

There are legal issues to consider. For example, the property may be restricted to residential use only. If you are buying a property, check there isn't a covenant that restricts its use as a place of business. In a rented property, it might be necessary to get the landlord's permission to set up shop. Depending on your discipline, there may be legal requirements or restrictions on the room you practise in. For example, acupuncturists are required to have a sink in their work space.

The ideal situation

Finding a quiet, private space at home is not always as easy as it sounds! The ideal situation would be to have a separate room with its own private entrance - a basement flat for example. Consider this if you are buying a home and planning to set up your practice there.

A private entrance to the therapy room will provide you with a strictly business area, one that is seperate from the rest of the house. The importance of this depends on the sort of therapy you practise. For counsellors, a shared entrance may contaminate transference issues. Members of your family might have to sneak about trying to avoid meeting your clients! A private entrance is also easier to keep neat and tidy and will promote a more professional image. On the other hand, a shared entrance with all the usual homely clutter can create a more relaxed and friendly environment. The decision is yours, you decide what you are most comfortable with for your practice.

The main benefits to working at home are saving money and the flexibility. You choose your working hours; on the other hand, it can be an enormous invasion of your private space. Careful planning will help avoid too much disruption, but you do need room to spare.

It's great not to have to travel to work, but the downside can be a flabby waistline and poor health due to lack of exercise. So keep doing those push ups.

Working From a Holistic Health Centre

Working from a centre has many advantages: there is no intrusion into your own home; it may look more professional; the centre may provide clients for you; you may gain more space; you don't have to keep your room at home tidy and things hidden away; you can meet and talk to other practitioners.

Working from a centre involves renting a room for a preset period of time, which can be expensive because you have to pay whether you have a client during that time or not. It can be difficult to cover costs, especially in the early days when you are still building up your clientele.

Some centres may be open to negotiation and may make a deal with you. For example, during your first month you could agree to pay only when you use the room for a session, or they may agree to deduct a percentage of your actual earnings. Striking such a deal would give you a bit of breathing space while you work on establishing yourself.

If you cannot come to an agreement with the centre, try enforcing a cancellation cost (tricky to implement unless people pay in advance) in case a client does not show up. Money issues, including cancellation fees are a part of the contract that needs to be established in the first session.

Which Hours?

You need to decide when it is best to rent the room. Check what the centre's opening hours are. Some places are open seven days a week and late into the evenings, giving you more opportunity to work.

The busiest and most profitable hours will be evenings after six o'clock and weekends. These slots may often been snapped up by other practitioners. Find out what is available and if this is likely to change in the near future. If the best hours for you are already booked, you might be able to go on a waiting list.

When booking a room, find out if anyone is using it directly before or after you. Using a room back-to-back with other practitioners can create a problem if you need time to set up and clear away equipment, or if you need to spend a bit of extra time with a client. In this case, consider renting some extra time.

Advertising

For someone starting their career, working at a centre can be ideal because the centre may provide clients for you and you can ask the management about mentioning you in their promotional literature.

Some centres do expect you to find your own clients. If this is the case you will need to advertise and promote yourself, preferably before renting the room, otherwise it could get very expensive! Leave leaflets at the centre advertising that you will be working there (for more ideas, see the section on promotion).

Reputation

It is worth doing a bit of research before making any commitments. Find out about the centre's reputation; working at a centre with a good reputation will help ensure you get lots of clients and will protect your own credibility. It will also give an air of professionalism to your practice. Good centres will ask for copies of your certificates and insurance papers and may only let you practice if you are a member of a professional therapy organisation.

Services Provided

Centres often provide reception services. You will need arrange with them how they should go about booking your new clients in. You will also have to establish whether they will call you when you have a new booking or if you will have to *check in* with them regularly to find out.

A reception provides added security and there are usually people about to turn to for help if you need it.

The centre you choose should have a waiting room and toilets. Some centres will even provide equipment such as massage tables, towels and tissues. Check out exactly what is being offered and that it is of a satisfactory standard, clean and safe!

Make sure that you can bring your own belongings, and set up the room as you like. If you keep patients' records you'll need a safe, secure place to leave these, rather than carting them around with you.

One of the best things about working at a holistic health centre is meeting the other practitioners. Such a network of people can be very supportive and encouraging (and you could swap treatments with each other). Other practitioners may refer clients to you if they are overbooked or feel you could provide a more suitable treatment. Centres do vary, however, in how much opportunity practitioners get to meet each other. If it is very important to you to have contact with colleagues, find out if the centre has practitioner meetings or a communal kitchen.

If you find that business is really picking up, you could start to work with some of your more regular customers at home rather than renting more time (although some centres don't like you doing this).

Although it is expensive and the working hours are inflexible, you may find that you prefer renting a room at a centre rather than working from home. Having your domestic space free from business can more than compensate for the drawbacks. Besides, your neighbours won't get spooked by all the comings and goings.

Working from a Medical Surgery or Clinic

Doctors are increasingly open to natural therapies. Many GPs study acupuncture, homeopathy and hypnotherapy. Often group practices have *in-house* counsellors.

To approach your local GPs, compile a list from the yellow pages, phone the surgery and find out the name of the practice manager. Write to this person and send your CV with a covering letter. In your covering letter, it is best to use a medical, clinical approach: offer treatments for particular medical conditions (for example, aromatherapy for relief of asthma or Thai massage for prenatal care). Follow up with a phone call a few days later.

When GPs refer to specialists, including counsellors and complementary medicine practitioners, they usually do so by letter and they expect a letter back. Your communication needs to be understood by your GP and your client needs to know about your communication. Good communication with a GP, verbal and in writing, without compromising your relationship with the client is a good way of attracting more referrals from that GP.

Working Hours and Pay

Medical clinics are usually open during the day and early evening. Generally, a therapist will work from the clinic for a morning or day at a time, and these hours make working with doctors convenient, and a solution to the problem of working more evenings than you would like.

Many GP practices are 'fund-holders', meaning that they have control of their own budget, out of which they have to pay for referrals to specialists (NHS and private). Many practices now employ counsellors and acupuncturists who are paid out of the practice budget.

What is Provided?

At some surgeries, your working space may be rather makeshift. Funds are low and rooms may not be designed to suit your needs. However, there will be a receptionist, a waiting room and security provided – not to mention clients!

Problems can arise if you find yourself disagreeing with orthodox treatments. You need to think about whether you can work happily alongside an approach which includes prescribed drugs and surgery. Before starting work at a clinic, you also need to remember that you may not have much choice about the clients you see. If you decide that you can live with these problems, you will find working in a medical surgery gives your practice an air of authority.

Renting in Other Locations

Often your local gym will be interested in offering a new service to their customers. A good massage and a sauna go very well together. Body builders can be interested in balancing their muscle-building exercises with yoga stretches. If you don't want to work at home and there's a gym just around the corner, it can be a convenient alternative.

Big hotels often have a fitness centre or gym. Remember local council leisure centres too. If you live in a tourist area, holiday camps will be a good place to look for potential clients.

Practising 'On Location'

Practising *on location* means that you go to your clients rather than your clients coming to you. This an option that only some therapists can take advantage of. It is relevant for practitioners of body therapies (massage, reflexology and reiki for example) and other portable practices like tarot card reading. It is unusual for counsellors and psychotherapists to practice in this way.

The mobile approach can open up the market for you, enabling you to reach clients that might otherwise be inaccessible. There are various things to consider when making house and company calls.

House Calls

House calls enable you to reach people who are unable to leave their home or prefer not to. This applies to disabled clients, people who are temporarily home bound due to injury, sickness or old age and people with young children. Some people just prefer to be treated at home because they find it more comfortable and relaxing, for instance, pregnant women and babies (*The National Childbirth Trust Newsletter* is a great way of accessing this market).

Working with people in their own home can be great. They will be more relaxed and open and will have at hand their favourite music or incense. They will also be able to stay warm and floppy at home rather than having to travel immediately after their treatment.

Counsellors don't usually make house visits, but you don't have to take convention as a rule. Alfred Adler used to visit clients in their own homes and some family and child psychotherapists still do so.

Costs and Equipment

Making house calls involves a lot of travelling and this has to be accounted for in the cost of the treatment; on the other hand, you won't have extra rent or heating bills to pay.

Having your own transportation is vital, unless all you need to carry is a deck of tarot cards. Lugging a massage table around on the bus is not much fun! Vehicle expenses incurred as a result of your business travel are tax deductible.

A mobile phone could be a useful and worthwhile expense; you will be constantly in touch with your clients, and you will be able to take bookings at any time.

Keep in mind that all your travel costs, meals out and other business expenses are tax deductible, so keep receipts!

Risks

There are obvious risks involved in going into a stranger's home. It is important to be aware of these and to take some precautions. Leave the address of where you are working with a colleague so that they know where to start looking if you go missing

Company Visits

Many companies are full of busy, stressed out people. Your mobile practice will offer these companies a quick, convenient, and stress reducing service. Depending on what type of therapy you practice, you could provide anything from neck and shoulder massages to counselling on interpersonal skills.

One of the advantages of taking your therapy to a company (as opposed to someone's house) is that personal security is not an issue since there are always people milling about.

Some companies now have EAP (employee assistance programme) schemes. This means that employees can have up to six sessions with a counsellor at the company's expense. This service is provided by a number of regional and national EAP providers. If you are a fully-qualified counsellor you can register with one of the providers and get your referrals through them.

Getting Started

Phone up prospective companies to find out the name of the person who can deal with your enquiry. Send a brochure and covering letter stating the useful service you can provide to them. Explain how it would make their staff work so much more efficiently and that this sort of thing is popular with many companies in the region. Companies will take you on if they think that their employees will work more productively, so *do* stress how the benefits of your therapy will increase sales or productivity, and make for a more contented work force.

Perhaps a few newspaper cuttings would help you make your point. 'High stress' businesses are the obvious places to target (for example, recording studios or people glued to VDU's). The personnel managers of bigger companies would be the person to approach initially.

Costs and Equipment

Although there will be some travel costs, they will not amount to much if you are targeting numerous clients at each company. As with making house calls, you won't have to pay rent or heating bills; and again, having your own car is essential if you need to carry heavy equipment about.

For masseurs, there are specially designed massage chairs available that are ideal for this sort of work: the client remains clothed and is perfectly positioned in the chair for you to give a thorough relaxing massage.

Working Hours

You will be probably be working during the day if you have to catch people while they are at work. At certain companies you may only be able to work with people during their lunch break, but if the office operates a flexible time system you should be able to see clients throughout the day.

Appropriate Therapies

Not all treatments will be appropriate for taking on location to a place of business. For example, oil massage could be tricky because it requires that the client get undressed, you would need a private space to work in and the client would have to go back to work with an oily body under their clothing (although some may enjoy this, not many would be comfortable with it).

A good rule of thumb when taking your therapy to a company is that the client remains clothed. Reflexology is ideal (shiatsu and Thai massage also work well but you need a bit of space to work in).

Raves and Clubs

Big clubs are increasingly interested in offering a variety of services alongside music and dancing. Many big raves have stalls selling a range of products from luminous clothes to healing crystals, and there are sometimes therapies on offer. However, working at raves is quite controversial. Some therapists dispute how effectively you can treat people in such a situation. Some people are on drugs and the atmosphere can be odd. The noise can be impossibly distracting and you will be up all night working with hot sweaty people.

That said, working at a rave can be great fun, especially if you like the music; you can boogie when you get fed up of working. However, not all therapies are suitable for practising at raves. Massage is a good treatment to give (although whatever you are practising, it is best to work on a table to avoid being stepped on). Offer small treatments: twenty minutes is enough to give someone a relaxing massage and an idea of what it's all about. If you can't imagine treating someone in that time frame, forget it. Or perhaps, like me, you are past it, and would rather see out your twilight years in a more sedate environment.

Setting Your Fees

Valuing Yourself

Many practitioners have trouble setting fees. You may feel that simply charging enough to cover your time and costs will mean setting your fees too high. But you must remember that you are offering private, specialist health care. You have to work very hard to provide this service and often work unsociable hours. It costs a lot of money to train in your therapy initially and then run your own business.

Your business depends on pricing yourself right: price yourself too low and you'll go bankrupt, price yourself too high and you won't attract enough clients to keep yourself in business. It's really a question of finding a balance.

Elasticity of Demand

One simple way of looking at it is *elasticity of demand*. The more people there are practising your particular brand of therapy, the less you will be able to charge; meanwhile, the fewer therapists there are practising your 'speciality', the more you can charge. It's not quite that simple, but that is a rough guide to looking at appropriate pricing for what you offer.

Setting fees is based on how much worth your customer sees in the service you offer, and this directly affects how much they are willing to pay for it.

Unsociable Hours

The hours you work will often be unsocial, and your fees should reflect this. Few of your clients will want to see you during the daytime. Much of your work will be done when the rest of the working population has finished work, during evenings and weekends. This will interfere with your social life. For example, you may find that everyone wants a treatment after work and that you are constantly torn between working and seeing friends. If you have children, you may find that your work prevents you from spending as much time with them as you'd like.

You are your own boss. If you are not happy with the hours you are working then stop and think. Perhaps you are targeting the wrong sort of client with your advertising. You can aim to attract people who are available during the hours you would prefer to work. Women with children, unemployed, retired people and so on.

Three Methods

Consider the three main ways that you can set your fees: the accountant's, the paranoid's, and the optimist's.

The Accountant's Way

The accountant's way of setting fees is to calculate your expenses, your basic costs, and add on the basic wage that you want to earn. This will give you your total desired income, and a basic rate that you have to charge each client. It will also give you an idea of the minimum number of clients you must see in order to earn your desired income.

Let's look at this on a weekly basis. If your business expenses (which should allow for expenses like advertising costs and office supplies that are not necessarily paid out on a weekly basis) for the week are £50 and your wage (that is, the money you need to earn to cover your personal expenses such as rent, food, etc.) is £200, then you have to earn a total of £250. So, if you are seeing ten clients a week, then you have to charge £25 per client - very simple! Of course, it's more sensible to calculate your budget on an annual basis, to ensure that it reflects reality as accurately as possible.

The major disadvantages of using this method are that it really isn't sensitive to the marketplace and that it doesn't really allow for expansion other than through a very well thought out increase in your rates.

The Paranoid's Way

The paranoid's way of setting their fees is to look at the competition, see how much they're charging, and to set your fees accordingly.

Obviously with this method you are going to have to set your price as low as them, or lower if you are looking to undercut them.

This is a great way to quickly go bankrupt, or at best it's a philosophy for 'getting by', because unless all of your competition is charging extravagant prices, you will set your prices too low and not be able to cover your costs.

The Optimist's Way

This is probably the best method: it is market sensitive, and should enable you to make more money than you would by setting your fees the accountant's way. Instead of seeing how much you need to earn, or how much other therapists are charging, this method is about finding out, through careful examination of the marketplace, how much your clients are willing to pay.

Let's explore a product found on supermarket shelves to explain this point. A can of baked beans varies in price from 4p to 24p. Heinz generally costs the most and no-name brands cost the least, but if you examine any two different brands closely, you will find that the list of ingredients is almost identical. However, people are perfectly willing to buy Heinz beans rather than the no-name brands. Why is this? Well, people are willing to pay more for a product for a variety of reasons: quality, difference, reputation, safety etc.

To justify the extreme price difference, Heinz executives claim to offer beans that are better and taste better than any other brand. Has anyone has ever seen this claim on their products? In actual fact, by charging more, Heinz are communicating a message that their beans are worth more without having to say it.

The moral of this story is that you can charge more than the competition. Far more in some cases! Price is not the only issue when it comes to choice. Price is determined by value. Clients will pay more if they value the therapy more.

Setting your pricing the optimist's way has the added advantage of more flexibility. Pricing can then become part of your marketing strategy. For example, if you were to create a new therapy (hint, hint), set your fees quite high initially and as other therapists come along who practise that therapy, you can bring your fees down to compete. This happens a lot with products: look at computers for example. When a new computer comes out it costs a couple of hundred pounds more than older models, but three months later as rival companies bring out similar models the price of our original model goes through the floor.

You may decide to set your fees very low initially, hoping to gain a large number of clients and keep out the competition, planning to put your fees up later when you have secured your reputation within the market. This is a risky strategy and you must use careful judgement if you adopt it.

Discounts and Concessions

Setting a higher price enables you to come down in price if you need to. You can offer discounts and concessions and may be able to negotiate a favourable outcome, such as 'Well I can see you at a reduced fee if you can come in the day'. Generally it's good policy that if you make a concession, you get something in return.

Negotiating

You may decide as a matter of course to set your prices high and come down when negotiating with potential clients. You could start at £39 for instance and come down to your lowest price of £29 and be willing to do this on a regular basis. Your clients will end up feeling they are getting value for money when they beat you down in price. This is a somewhat risky venture, because it's not like selling a car when you start selling at a high price and come down. After all you will not see this person again, whereas your clients will come on a regular basis and may find out how much your other clients are paying. If they are paying £35 and another is only paying £29, you may be asked to justify the price difference to them.

It's much harder to put prices up than to bring them down. So think twice before setting your fees low. When you do increase your prices, you will need to justify the price increases. 'It's to keep pace with inflation' is easier for your clients to accept than 'I need the money, I've been undercharging'. Otherwise they are likely to re-evaluate your worth to them.

So, its seems best to err on the wrong side of pricing too high than too low, as you can always come down a bit. It is also important to take into account the cost of marketing your business, and generally practitioners tend to underestimate the cost of promotion.

Price Plateaux

It's no accident that goods are often priced at £9.99, £4.99, £19.99. This is called a price plateaux, and, although it seems a rather obvious and simple strategy, it is used because it works. It may be the difference of only a penny, but there is something about going over the threshold of a fiver or twenty pounds that creates some sort of psychological barrier.

If you charge £30 a session, why not try £29. It's not much less for you, but it can make a big difference when seen through a client's eyes. Consider reducing the time of a session: if you were to bring your prices down from £30 to £29 and work a fifty-minute hour instead of one hour, you will have effectively put your prices up by 16%.

Some practitioners, however, believe that £9.99 or whatever, does not befit the healing scene and gives the impression of a supermarket pricing structure. As there are no hard and fast rules, it's up to you to make your own judgements.

Buyer's Remorse

You have probably experienced buyer's remorse yourself when you have bought an expensive item and got it home. You might have wondered while you were paying by cheque or credit card if you were doing the right thing. This is *buyer's remorse*. You go through feelings of anxiety; 'maybe I should take it back' or 'I shouldn't have bought this, I can't afford it', 'I'm sure this is the wrong thing for me'. You are filled with guilt. Can you really afford it?

Similarly, your clients when they sign up with you and write their first cheque go through the same thing. They may get home and have the same doubts. What they've bought is a number of sessions or the promise of a number of sessions, and it costs a lot of money. They too may be filled with remorse and wonder if they've done the right thing or have spent too much money, or wonder if they can afford it, or if it will really do them any good. And it is easy for them to cancel, all they have to do is pick up the phone and say 'I don't think I can afford it'. Or 'I don't think it is right for me'.

The first session is an assessment session. At the end of the first session you need to have a formulation, a therapy plan and a prognosis. These you need to share with the client, so that the process is clear and you are both happy and agreed on a plan.

What do manufacturers do to counter buyer's remorse? When you open up the package the product has to look good, shine and work properly. On top of that they have notes that say things like 'Congratulations, You are the proud owner of...'

They state how and why the product is so good and why you've made the right choice in buying it. Furthermore, they offer after-sales backup, and provide a phone number of their customer services who are there to help you. If you have a problem you can phone them and they will reassure you and tell you what to do. This ensures that you don't return the equipment.

In a similar way you must offer an after-sales service. You must listen to what your remorseful client has to say when they phone up. If they want to cancel, find out why, even if you can't change their mind. It is useful to listen to what they have to say for future reference so that you can improve your strategy. It is easy, when someone phones up to cancel, to become defensive or annoyed, or even so angry that you slam down the phone. It's better to try and avoid this. Put aside your feelings of rejection and hurt and listen to what their problem is - you might learn something useful. They may say ' I've decided I can't afford it'. This usually means that they feel they are not getting value for money. Talk about their doubts. Talking it through with them is good feedback for you and in the process you might change their mind.

You may also consider the notes of congratulations that manufacturers use to promote their products and to ease the anxieties. Clients also need this pat on the back. They need to feel what they've done is right and you can deliver this message to them.

It may be something to do with their expectations not being met. After all if you have designed a slick, glossy brochure and they go to your premises which are a dirty, run down, feeble mess, there is obviously a difference between your presentation in your brochure and what you deliver. It may be that in your promotional literature you promise one thing but fail to really touch on that in your initial sessions. For instance, it could be that you promise bio-energetic body work. A client comes to see you and you simply talk for that first session. The client may be wondering 'Will I ever get to do bio-energetics or are we going to talk about it forever? This may be a reason for them dropping out.

Many people drop out of therapy in the initial stages and it is very important to learn why by listening to what they say. It may be worth phoning them up if they've just left a message on your answer phone to cancel. If you can bear it, give them a ring and talk it through with them.

In trying to find out why they've dropped out, don't be too quick to frame it in your own ideas of why - it's very easy to be defensive when getting this kind of feedback. When you've listened to what they have to say and put the phone down you can think over the conversation.

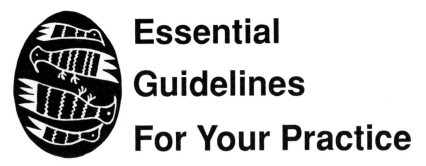

Essential Guidelines For Your Practice

1. Location is Crucial

It is of crucial importance that your practice or centre is within a reasonable distance from locations where potential or existing clients live and work. This is especially true if you intend to get clients from the local community. What you consider to be your local community depends on the area you live in. If you live in a densely-populated area, like London, then you might consider your local community to be within a five-mile radius. Your clients will come from within this area. If you live in a more sparsely populated, rural area then you will have to consider a larger area. Clients will come from further afield, maybe from twenty or forty miles around.

The fewer obstacles in the way of your potential clients, the more likely they are to come to you on a regular basis. A major obstruction for any client is having to take time off to travel. Time and cost of travel can seriously put potential clients off. People will probably look for someone who is practising closer to them if you are located too far away.

Potential clients will be prepared to travel if you are offering something that is very unusual or unique or that very few other practitioners are doing. If you are offering a very specialised course or therapy then your clients will have no choice but to come to you, wherever you are!

However, the holistic field is presently mushrooming. Other practitioners will almost inevitably pop up in your area and this has to be taken into account. If you are running workshops the situation is somewhat different, because the clients will be more willing to travel to a workshop where they will be for a whole day or two or a week. The journey time will be less significant if they are to spend a longer period of time with you. The travelling time, as a proportion of the therapy time, is much smaller with a workshop than with an individual session of an hour or so.

Locating your practice in a high-density area of clients means you are more likely to keep your clients. Clients are more likely to drop out if they have to travel long distances on a regular basis. This can be avoided if a good rapport is established, or clients have made some sort of an investment in the therapy. If you practise a therapy with a high turnover of clients, and they only come for a small number of sessions they may be willing to travel for that period. For example if you do massage and your clients come to you for six sessions, some clients may not mind travelling to you for this short period of time. If you are looking for long term clients then the time and costs of travel play a more major role as an obstacle to potential clients.

2. Identify Who Your Potential Clients Are

Firstly you must have a good idea of what your potential client is like. This can be based on the kind of client you are looking for. If you are offering a service that is aimed at ethnic minorities then you need to locate your practice where they live or work. If you are offering family therapy you want to locate in a residential area where there is a high proportion of families.

If you don't have an area of specialisation, then you have to determine on a much more general level, what your potential client is like. You can do this by using your own knowledge and experience of what they are like and by asking other practitioners who offer a similar service to your own.

Questions to ask are; Are they married? Single? Male? Female? High income? Low income ? Disposable income? Between what ages? And so on. This will give you some idea of who the typical clients who come to your therapy are likely to be. Knowing who they are will enable you to locate them and to locate your practice.

In general, a typical client seeking therapy tends to be middle class, female, reasonably well off, without children, living in owner occupied or shared accommodation. She will read either the Guardian, Independent, Sunday Times, Sunday Observer. Quite often having children can present an obstacle to doing therapy. If the potential client is the main child carer, then they will need a babysitter. The cost of the babysitter will be an additional expense, unless they have a partner who can look after the child. It is less likely that people with children will do therapy. The example above is a gross generalisation, of course. The reality that is that the market is *segmented* and there is a different profile for each segmentation. (See chapter *A Quick Guide to Marketing* for a discussion of segmentation.)

To paint a more true-to-life picture of your potential client you must obtain as much information on them as possible. There may not be one type, you may find there are a cluster of different types. It is a good idea to go to the locations where you intend to set up practice to see if your type of client is there.

If you are planning to set up or run a centre and are thinking of relocating, you could use a marketing company to provide you with a demographic breakdown of certain areas. Marketing companies provide this service for a fee. You need to provide them with a profile of the typical client that you are looking for. They draw on a large database that can do a sophisticated analysis and provide you with numbers and places where your potential clients are likely to live. It is an expensive service and probably outside the bounds of what an individual practitioner can afford. The fees are likely to be in the region of several hundred pounds to cover several hundred square miles. These private marketing companies are used by large companies (especially franchises like MacDonald's and Dixon's). It is important to do the research before you locate yourself somewhere. Local libraries will have information about these marketing companies. You will find information about them under *market research*.

3. Avoid Competition

When locating your practice, you must consider the competition. You want to set up your practice where there are few other similar practitioners to avoid this competition for clients. Go to the area and look in places where leaflets are displayed, health centres, clinics, community centres, libraries and so on to get an idea of who else practices in the area and what they are doing.

A quick look at the *Yellow Pages* will give you some idea of the number of practitioners in the area. You can look in local magazines and newspapers to see what is on offer and if there are any centres or individual practitioners offering the same things as you are. The more unique your service, the better. For example, if you are a reflexologist and want to move to Manchester, you should find out how many other reflexologists Manchester has. If there is an overabundance of them, you might want to reconsider the move.

The exception to this rule is when the service in the area has generated a lot of interest and increased the demand for it. This does happen. For example, in cities a lot of shops offering similar products are located in close proximity. In London, there are a lot of tailors on Saville Row and they generate enough interest to support all of them despite the competition.

You have to use a certain amount of your own common sense and knowledge to decide whether the market will sustain another therapist in an area of high density.

The most effective way of avoiding competition is to uncover your uniqueness and promote it. This is detailed in the section *Your Uniqueness is Important* in this book.

4. Don't Wait to Be Discovered

There does seem to be a belief among practitioners that if they are good enough, clients will come banging on their door. This is not the case, so don't wait to be discovered. There are only two types of people who will beat a path to your door: people to whom you owe money, and people who are trying to sell you something. Notice that neither of these groups are likely to be potential clients. You have to get out there and find those clients and work hard at attracting them to you.

The most successful practitioners tend to have good business and marketing skills. They are able to use these skills and abilities to further their practice. So if you find that you are having difficulty in getting more clients, perhaps you need to put more work into your marketing, promotion and publicity. You are probably a great practitioner, but you need to develop your business skills.

Being a good practitioner is only half of the answer. Having the right business skills is the other half. If you ask other practitioners how they get more clients and they say 'they just seem to come to me', it is likely to be nonsense! They may be getting clients because of their ability to sell themselves to people they speak to. Perhaps they talk a lot about their clients and mention how successful they are with them. All the listeners want to sign up on the spot. This sort of self publicity is a business skill. Thus they promote themselves without realising it.

28

When we first published our book *Holistic London*, and had them delivered from the printer, they were left sitting on our living room floor. There was nowhere else to store them and we were forced to stack in the form of settee, an arm chair and a table. This made them at least valuable until we could decide what to do with them. We knew we had a good book and we knew there was a demand for it. I had this fantasy that the book was so good that, like gold mining, there would sooner or later be a rush to find us. Then, a day later, like a lightning bolt, I realised we had to sell them, because no one was going to come knocking on the door to buy them! My first thought was that we had to sell them to book shops. At least this would get them into the shops. But then how would the public know what book to ask for when in the shop? So we had to publicise it and promote it. A lot of work had to go into promotion and publicity for the book. The business skills I learnt from this became essential and invaluable in building up the business. Since then I've learnt a lot more about how to market, promote and sell books.

5. Target Your Potential Clients

Aim promotion and publicity at where your clients are, where they live and work or where they read. Don't just go and put a notice up in your local newsagent and expect to get clients from that. Rather than spending a fortune on advertising, think of reducing your advertising budget. Advertising in local specialist publications that your potential clients are likely to read, is cheaper and more effective than general advertising. If you want to run a course that is aimed at practitioners of complementary medicine, you need to think about how you can reach practitioners of complementary medicine. Think about what publications they are likely to read, find a mailing list of them, insert a leaflet in the appropriate publications. This targeting is a very effective way of advertising and promoting yourself. You might find a list of centres where they practice, or a list of training centres that they might have attended.

6. Allow Time and Money for Marketing

I know it's not what you want to do, but any successful business must have a sales department, and you have to be your own. You must be able to sell, market and promote yourself *in addition to* finding out where the clients are. This takes time and money and must be reflected in the fees you charge. If you don't account for the costs of marketing in your fees, you will find that you don't have enough money to market yourself properly. It's a downward spiral.

Conversely, if you put a lot of time and money into marketing, you will get more clients. When you have the clients, you'll have the money for even more extensive marketing.

This book is just the start in telling you how to go about marketing effectively. It covers all the essential points, now however, you have to put your thus-far dormant marketing genius into action! Put aside time to work out a budget for your business. (It will make your bank manager happy and help you form a sense of stability about your business) Ideally, you will lose that sense of riding the roller coaster of clients. You are high when you have a full clientele and low when your client load is low. You need to get off the roller coaster; and devoting more time to marketing, promotion and publicity will help you do just that.

7. Make Yourself Available

Many practitioners hide away and clients have to go to great lengths to find them. This may show itself by omitting their phone numbers on their adverts and expecting people to write to them instead. It can result in them pretending that they don't really need clients. Some practitioners feel they need to employ a strategy of appearing to have a full clientele in order to attract clients. The downside of this is they cannot mention they need clients to others who may be able help find them. It is essential that you make yourself available and easily contactable and are prepared to sell yourself to your clients. You should treat each and every incoming call as a sale. See it as a potential client trying to reach you and put every effort into convincing them to come and visit you. Don't expect your clients to have to put too much energy into finding you.

8. Find Out How People Find Out About You

Ask your clients how they heard about you. Make a note of this and keep a log of where they are coming from. If they picked up a leaflet, ask them where they found it. You can make the address on adverts slightly different from your own address so that if people respond in writing you will know where they heard about you.

It is very easy to overestimate the rate at which your business will grow. Remember that your response rate for advertising will be, depending on how you advertise, probably less than 1%. For example, if you distribute a thousand leaflets, you are likely to get ten responses and perhaps just one client. Don't let this put you off, you will just have to do a lot more and build this time and work into your costs.

It is very common for practitioners to underestimate the amount of publicity they need to run a successful business. You need to do a lot and in a variety of ways. You don't need to spend a lot. It is easy to waste a lot of money on advertising. You need to work out your budget in detail. Establish whether you are spending your money on the right kind of marketing strategies.

Once you discover which avenues are working for you in terms of promotion, you can then concentrate your budget on the most effective ones. This is essential for learning for the long-term health of your business.

9. Listen to Your Clients

Marketing is all about supplying needs. It is very much dominated by the economic rule of supply and demand. If you find out what your clients need, you will be in a much better position to supply it. This can happen on a one-to-one basis with your existing or potential clients by asking them what they need or want. Of course, ideally your clients will tell you their needs without any prompting. It may be that you can offer a particular service if you have enough demand. If enough clients come to you with similar symptoms you can offer a service to satisfy this demand and make this part of your publicity and promotion. If lots of your clients come to you specifically for treatment of headaches, then you can gear your promotion towards headache relief, for instance. If 'relationship with a partner' is a prime focus for many of your clients, consider running a workshop on this subject.

10. Build Up A Solid System for Finding Clients

There are many ways of finding clients. Eliminate the ones that don't work and build upon the ones that do. It may be that your clients come from a referral centre down the road; you may get clients from advertising in certain publications; from responses to leaflets. Find out which ones work. Build upon this system and hone it down. Discover by trial and error which leaflets are working and which ones are not. Improve upon the leaflets that don't work. Perhaps you can change the style, the colour or the headline. Build on the leaflets that *do* work and use those. If you are being referred clients by a centre, keep in touch with the centre and maintain that relationship. Referral channels need continual maintenance.

11. Use Former Clients for Referrals

As with advertising, it is crucial to maintain those avenues which are effective for bringing in clients, and eliminate those that aren't. Former clients can be a wonderful source of referrals, but you need to concentrate your efforts on those who will respond.

Mail your past and present clients with your leaflets and flyers about workshops, courses and demonstrations that you are offering. This is the best way to spread the word about what you are doing, not just to re-attract old clients, but to attract their families, friends and associates. This can prove particularly effective if your past clients speak well of you. There is nothing like clients promoting you and saying how great they think you are. Give your former clients special consideration in your publicity.

12. Over-Publicise Yourself

Generally practitioners do too little publicity and expect too much response from what they have done. Attracting clients takes a lot of work. Much time and energy has to be spent to get the *bums on seats* for any event.

For every leaflet that you put out a 1% response rate is good. So don't think that by producing 100 leaflets that you are going to get a big response, because you will probably get nothing.

13. Come Out of The Closet

You are going to have to promote and publicise yourself if you are going to be successful. Many practitioners market themselves in a small way and make promotion only a small part of what they do. They really hide themselves, don't get known and they fail.

I am not sure what causes this. It may be that fear of failure inhibits practitioners. It may be a fear of stepping into the limelight and having others judge them that stops them. It may be that they simply underestimate the amount of publicity they will need to become successful. Either way, not putting enough energy and resources into one's own publicity is a sure way to anonymity and failure.

14. Be Patient

It takes time to build up a client support network, that is, to build up a complex network of referrals and promotion that will continually feed you with clients. It may take years.

Your business will build up over time and you will get known over time. However, you cannot rely on just one or two methods of bringing in clients. The more avenues of promotion and networking you explore, the better your response rate will be. Don't expect this to happen overnight; developing this kind of client support network is particularly difficult if you are new to the field. You will make errors and learn from them. As long as you don't give up, your devotion to marketing will pay off.

You may find in time, that your former clients become your best source of referrals. It can take a long time to accumulate a substantial number of past clients.

15. Don't Move Premises

Relocating your premises makes it difficult for potential clients to get in touch with you, especially if they have old leaflets or literature. You really must stay in one location over a long period to gain a critical mass of past clients.

However, you may find that you don't want to stay in the same place for a long time and one way out of this is to get a phone number that moves with you. There are companies offering this service. You can also use a *mailing address* and phone number that remains constant. This is especially useful if you are living in rented accommodation and are not sure how long you will be there or where you will be next.

16. Professional Inhibitions

Just because you are a professional does not mean you don't need marketing skills. You may, however, feel 'cheap' to advertise yourself, but you don't need to compromise your professional standards to market yourself. Check if your professional organisation has guidelines for advertising. Check your personal blocks and work on the ones that are related to your fears and inhibitions, and don't forget, there are many people out there who you could help. They need to know about you.

A Quick Guide to Marketing

What is Marketing?

The very word *marketing* can be intimidating. There are uncomfortable connotations of the cut-throat world of advertising and promotion, of dishonesty and false claims. However, everyone in business today employs some form of marketing, even if they are not aware of it.

So let's define marketing as the philosophy of what you do and what your business is. Marketing is about seeing your business through the eyes of your customers. It's about seeing what they need and providing a service that satisfies this need.

Marketing is about gearing your whole business towards providing a service that people want. It is anticipating what your customers might need in the future and providing the right service for them at the right time. This is more of an art than a science. The most successful marketing expert often works from equal parts intuition and research.

Another aspect of marketing that many therapists are very adept at lies in recognising the constantly changing nature of the work that they do, and the constantly changing aspect of the market. Markets do change. For instance, it may be that your particular therapy has bad press: the media says that your particular brand of therapy is of poor quality and the people working in it are badly trained. If this is the case, you need to be receptive to your clients' concerns towards these issues. Indeed, you need to take this into account in your promotional material, and in the way that you deal with your clients in regard to these particular issues.

One of the many criticisms levelled against marketing departments in large organisations is that they don't listen to their customers enough. You, on the other hand, are running your own small business and you are constantly in touch with your clients and know what their needs are. Actually, it may appear to you that you know what they want but it's always worth listening rather than being too quick to judge.

Where is The Market?

I've used the term *marketplace* before, but there really is no such thing. A market is made up of endless *segments*. A marketing expert's job is to identify particular segments or groups of the population with the same particular needs.

Two useful ways for therapists to divide the market by are: geography (where people live and work) and customer type (this is used for aiming at a particular type of clients). The analysis of customer type can be endlessly broken down.

For instance, if you are a massage practitioner you want to look for people who want massage, but you are going to have to narrow that field down a little further if you want to effectively target a group in your advertising. So, you decide to look for people who want massage because they have high-stress jobs. Narrowing it down a little more, you may want to give massage to people who are in high-stress jobs and suffer specifically from neck and shoulder pains.

This type of segmentation means that you reach a smaller number of people, but that you will reach the people who are more likely to become clients. You'll probably find that there are different segments of the population that you can effectively target.

Segmentation

An example of segmentation can be seen in laundry detergent. Basically the idea of laundry detergent is that it washes things clean, and it makes them white. Pretty simple, right? However, you'll find that some will claim to soften the fabric further, others will offer a biological (as opposed to non-biological) cleaning process, others are specifically made for washing delicate items by hand, some have special ingredients added that will provide resistance towards stains - the list goes on forever. Just go to the supermarket and view the selection of laundry detergents on offer, you will see that each one targets a specific market segment even though they are all essentially the same product. Think about it the next time you buy detergent: even if you are not aware of it, you are buying the one that appeals the most to your particular habits and preferences.

From now on you should think of segmentation describing what you offer. For example, if you offer counselling, remember that there are a lot of counsellors out there. It's no good just offering counselling, counsellors are two-a-penny and you will find yourself competing with them all. You have got to offer something that differentiates you. Not only that, but you must aim at a particular customer need and a particular segment of the market.

Yuppies, Dinks, Woops, Etc.

In books on marketing you'll probably come across how social psychologists break markets down in terms of their class and income. This information is all a lot of fun but not of much use to you. As a matter of interest I'll mention a few of the terms used to describe certain socio-economic groups of the population, that is, people who share common cultural, economic and historical backgrounds. Most famously, there are the yuppies, who you probably know about. There are also DINK's (Double Income No Kids), WOOP's (Well-Off Older People), DUMP's (Desperately Under financed Mortgage Paupers), SWELL's (Successful Women Earning Lots of Lolly), SMARM's (Sophisticated Middle Aged Rejuvenated Marketing experts) and finally, YARGGS's (Young Aggressive Ruthless Go-Getters).

Identifying Your Client Market

Start by knowing who you want to work with. These are the people you are going to be working with and spending much of your time with. It is important that you are happy working with them. Do you want to work only with men or only with women? Do you want long term clients? Does this suit the sort of service you offer? Some practices (such as reflexology) have a large turnover of clients. If you are a counsellor do you want to work with very disturbed people?

Who and Where Are Your Clients

Who wants what you offer? If you offer a stress management service, you need to find people who are stressed. You need to be specific about what you offer. Who are the people that are going to benefit from what you have to offer? Be specific about who your potential clients are. Are they male or female? Are they young or old? What will their interests be? What newspapers will they read? Try to build up a clear picture of what your ideal client is like. Be clear and avoid generalising. Do they eat in whole food restaurants ? Do they visit art galleries? If you are specific in what you offer, you should have a good idea of where to find your clients.

For example, if you are teaching yoga, and would prefer to work with younger, more flexible people, think of where they would gather. You could distribute your leaflets to colleges and universities, pubs and clubs. If you practice Thai massage and find your treatments particularly effective for people who sit down all day, contact offices, temping agencies, transport offices (bus and tube drivers spend their whole working lives sitting down!) Once you know who your clients are, you can find out where they are.

Research Your Local Area

As many of your clients and potential clients live or work locally, it's important to be aware of relevant local events, shops and restaurants, galleries and centres that could be used for promotion. If you are new to the area, it's worth putting time into surveying the locality with your business in mind. Although you gain familiarity with the area while living there doing non-business related things, it's worth spending some time researching the area solely with promotion in mind.

A visit to the local library is a good place to start. They usually carry lots of information about the local area, such as local newspapers, magazines, leaflets, directories and quite often they have a notice board. While you are at the library you could do some promotion at the same time by putting a notice up on their notice board, or leaving some leaflets on display. If you find the librarian friendly and helpful, it's worth asking them for help and they may be able to suggest things you had not thought of. They can sometimes be mine of information with their local knowledge of the area and special-interest groups.

Your Uniqueness is Important

You are unique. What you do is unique. However, you may not think so. You may think you are one counsellor amongst many counsellors, one homoeopath amongst many homoeopaths, or one tarot reader amongst many tarot readers, with very little to separate you from the herd. If you believe this, it becomes very difficult to promote yourself because you do not have an identity that potential clients can relate to. Further, you are putting yourself in competition with other counsellors, homoeopaths and tarot readers. If you promote your uniqueness then there is no competition! Think of it. If you are unique, if you are the only one, then nobody can compete with you!

In the world of marketing the common term for this is USP (Unique Selling Proposition) and anyone selling a product or service will strive to make their products and services unique. Marketing experts will go much further than this and will attempt to create an illusion of uniqueness, even if there is not one, simply because of the value of uniqueness.

You do not have to pretend to be unique, you and what you do *are* unique. What do I mean by this? In selling their therapy, practitioners are not just selling a service, they are selling themselves; the way that they practice therapy is intrinsically bound up with who they are.

Developing Your Uniqueness the Easy Way

It's easy to discover your uniqueness by using the following method, borrowed from Personal Construct Therapy. This method is based on looking at how you and other practitioners are similar, and yet different, from each other.

1. Make a list of six practitioners (include yourself as one of these practitioners) who offer the same therapy as you. If you cannot think of six, then choose other practitioners who offer a similar therapy to you, until you have the required six individuals.

2. Make two columns on a piece of paper. Above one column write the heading *Similar* and head the other *Different.*

3. Select three names from the list, and think about how one is different from the other two. (You do not have to include yourself in the three individuals you have chosen.) Write this down as one short sentence (even one word will suffice) under to *Different* column. Write down how the remaining two individuals are similar in the other column.

4. Choose another three from the list. These three must not be exactly the same as the first three, at least one must be different. Again think about how one is different from the other two, and how the other two are similar to each other and write this down.

5. Do step four above another four times. You should now have six ways in which the practitioners are different from and similar to each other.

6. Look through the list and decide which phrases best describe you and what you do.

7. Now develop a self description from this to form the basis for your promotional literature.

Example - Jane the Massage Therapist

Here is an example. Let's pretend you are Jane, a massage practitioner. You make a list of five other practitioners, Henrietta, Dave, Mike, Helen and Andrew.

You choose three from the list: Helen, Henrietta and Dave. You think that Henrietta is different because she uses a technique, whereas Helen and Dave practise intuitive massage.

You choose three from the list; Jane, Mike and Helen. You think that Mike is different from yourself (Jane) and Helen because he works on deep muscle tissue, whereas you and Helen have a lighter touch.

Choose another three from the list; Andrew, Mike and Dave. You think Dave is different from the other two because he uses essential oils, whereas Andrew and Mike don't.

You continue doing this until you have eight items (or constructs) laid out on a piece of paper as shown below.

How the two therapists are similar	How the other is different
Use a technique	Does intuitive massage
Work on deep muscle tissue	Has a light touch
Use essential oils	Does not use essential oils
Work with emerging emotions	Ignores emerging emotions
Aim for a long term benefit	Aims to relax the person for one day only
Work with the breath	Does not work with the breath
Charge big fees	Charges reasonable fees
Work with both sexes	Works with women only

Once you (Jane) have done this you need to decide which of these constructs best describes you. You look at the list and think: I do intuitive massage; my touch is light although I do dig deep sometimes;

I use essential oils; I work with emerging emotions; I aim for long term benefits; I do not work with the breath; I charge a reasonable fee; I only work with women.

Jane has now discovered why she is different from other massage practitioners! Even though she may already have had ideas of how she different, this is a systematic method which give comprehensiveness and clarity. The main benefit, however, is that is uses her own 'constructs', it uses her perspective, her own inner language and does not force anything upon her.

The next step is to develop a self description which will attract clients. Such a description could become part of her promotional literature.

Here is such a description:

Relax and Get Healthy

"When you totally relax you get healthy. Your body needs to unwind and I can offer the most relaxing massage with essential oils. Just one session is all that is needed to experience the benefits of deep relaxation.

Sometimes the body can hold chronic tensions and when these are encountered I can offer a deeper form of massage if you require it. Working on chronic tensions enables you to become forever free of those irritating aches and pains.

Even gentle massage can help release blocked feelings held in the body as tension. In a safe supportive environment these emotions can be let go of, leaving you relaxed, and with a deep sense of well being and confidence.

£25 per one-hour session. Women only.

Contact Jane on...

Example - Charles the Counsellor

Working from the steps listed in the last example Charles a counsellor develops the following constructs:

How the two therapists are similar	How the other is different
Focus on clients relationships	Focus is on anything the client wishes
Work with groups	Works with individuals
Give interpretations	Does not interpret
Trained in Gestalt Therapy	Trained in Jungian Therapy
Reveal self to clients	Remains 'opaque' in sessions
Sit on chairs	Sits on cushions
Focus on transference	Transference of minor importance
Show own feelings to client	Does not let clients see his emotions.

Charles, after looking at the list decides that he: focuses the therapy on his clients' relationships with others, works with individuals; gives interpretations; has a background in both Jungian and Gestalt Therapy; does not reveal himself to his clients; sits on chairs; focuses on transference; shows his own feelings to his clients if he feels it will help them.

Thus armed with this information Charles is able to write a brief self-description which he can use for promotional purposes as follows.

Being Real with People

Being yourself with other people is an art. Making and keeping friendships, and relating better to people at work, gives a sense of well being and increases your own self esteem.

I see individuals on a one-to-one basis to discuss and explore the many issues of relationships. By acting as a mirror to you, I can help you find your own path. I seek to clarify issues you will bring to the therapy, to put them in their perspective, and to find solutions.

Inevitably there will be times when we will need to focus on our own relationship as this can be a rich source of information. The way we relate to each other will, to some extent, be a reflection of how we relate to others. Working through and resolving any issues that may surface can lead to a satisfying and healthier way of relating to other people.

Contact Charles on...

Example - Diana the Tarot Reader

Working from the steps listed above, Diana develops the following constructs from a list of six tarot readers, including herself.

How the two therapists are similar	How the other is different
Use Rider Waite Tarot pack	Uses Crowley pack
Make wild guesses	Is intuitive
Do not predict the future	Predicts the future
Talk too much	Listens to client
Focus on life decisions	Focuses on whatever the client brings up
Make astrological connections	Does not bring astrology into the conversation
Wear stunning outfits	Wears normal clothes
Give excellent readings	Gives poor readings

After making this list Diana decides that she uses the Rider Waite pack; is intuitive; likes to focus on decisions the client might be struggling with; does not predict the future for the client; probably talks too much; makes astrological connections; has a stunning outfit that she is very proud of; her readings are consistently good. She then forms a description of herself as follows

I Have The Answer

Are you struggling with a question? Do you need to make a decision? Let the tarot provide the answer. The tarot is an ancient and tested tool for such an occasion. You do not have to say a word, let me do all the talking if you wish!

I use my intuitive skills in combination with the renowned sensitivity of the Rider Waite tarot pack. I focus not on the future, but on the mysteries of the present which holds the key to making the correct choice. There may be some astrological clues to your question, and if you would like we can combine these with the power of the tarot to find the answer for you.

Contact Diana on...

Some Notes

1. You do not have to limit yourself to only eight constructs. You can use more if you need to.

2. To gain a wider variety of constructs try using practitioners who do not practice the same discipline as you.

3. In your promotional literature, focus on the benefits of the constructs. For instance, in the example of Charles, the benefit of focusing on the client's relationships with other people 'gives a sense of well being and increases one's own self esteem'.

Presentation

These days people expect things to be less expensive and of better quality. There is no reason why the therapy business should be different. After all, if we are an advancing society, the healing techniques that we use should be quicker and more effective.

In many people's minds the society we live in promotes the attitude that quick means good and that modern medicine revolves around fast cures. We have been brought up on fast relief pain killers and antibiotics. We have numerous time-saving devices in our homes as time is precious, time is money and speed is essential. Alternative therapies work on a different philosophy and do involve time for healing and are not 'quick fixes'. Some practices will actually make you feel worse before you feel better.

The idea is that this sort of healing is deep and thorough and will not result in unpredictable side-effects that may pop up in two-years time or leave you with another problem. However, the reality is that people will be attracted to a treatment that has immediate results. If you tell them that it may take a long time to ease their problems they may feel you are just trying to get money out of them and will go to someone else.

Although you may be convinced that quicker is not necessarily better, you must remember that your clients probably think otherwise. If you want them to come to you will have to be careful about how you voice your beliefs. The business of counselling and psychotherapy can take years, there's no doubt about that. If your client is embarking on long-term counselling with you then they are about to spend a vast amount of money. They are going to need to feel that they've made the right choice and that you are doing your best to become more (and by the same token, speedier) in what you do.

A major weakness in psychotherapy is that it takes so long, so it's not a good idea to emphasise it. This may put people off. It's no selling point that psychotherapy takes years and costs a large fortune. The fact that it often lasts for years is actually a weakness, and it is something that your clients are very aware of.

Your potential clients will think to themselves (much as they would with a plumber or builder), "Well, if the therapist is bad, the process of therapy is going to take longer and longer and it will cost me more money. But the more effective the therapist is, the quicker I'll be able to sort out my problems and the less expensive it will be". Maybe this isn't entirely justified, but it *is* what many of your potential clients may be thinking.

Advertising and Promotion

Creating a Great Advert

Stress the Benefits

Your advertisement or leaflet should be dominated by the benefits of what you are offering. 'Sell the sizzle, not the sausage.' This should be reflected not only in the overall text, but also in the headline. It's a good idea to make out a list of the benefits of what you do, then write a full description for each of these benefits. Once you have done this you should have plenty of material from which to distil some good 'copy' (copy refers to the text of your advert or leaflet). This exercise will clarify for you some of the effects your skill has upon people.

Don't be tempted to use the name of your business or your logo as the headline as the largest element in your advert. This is a sure-fire way of sending it straight into the nearest bin. You may think it looks good to see your name in print, but it's uninteresting to most people. It's a good idea to make the headline something that crystallises the benefits of what you have to offer.

For example, 'A Cure for Backache' is much more interesting than 'Jones & Jones Ltd', particularly for those people who suffer from backache. You may think this is obvious, but take a look at the advertisements for centres and practitioners in magazines and you will find it's common for them to take the name of their centre as the headline! 'Relax with Ease' works better than 'Reflexology'. If you can think of a catchy headline then all the better.

Benefits and Features

The *benefits* of what you offer appeal to the emotional concerns of the reader. The *features* of what you do will appear to the intellect of the reader.

For example, the benefits of your therapy may be: relaxation, ability to relate better to others, healthier body, relief from worry etc., whereas features are: massage with oils, exploring basic rhythms of the body and that sessions last for an hour.

The benefits and features of your particular service will be mingled throughout the copy, there is no cut-and-dried approach to writing copy. Remember it's the benefits which catch the attention, so they should come first in the copy.

Be Unique

It's likely you have something that is unique in what you. Don't just stress that you are a counsellor, a Reiki practitioner or a tarot reader, you need to stress what it is that makes you unique from all the other counsellors, Reiki practitioners and tarot readers. Clients tend to pick up lots of leaflets and choose from one of them. Why should they choose from yours rather than another? If you don't know then you are lost, and are left competing with other practitioners on price and this is a costly way of competing and not very effective. Think about what it is that makes you different from all the other counsellors out there. Do you specialise in something? Do you aim to address particular needs in clients? Do you work with young people? If you are a tarot reader then have you been on television, do you use a special tarot pack? Do you focus on relationships? (See previous chapter for an exercise to help clarify your uniqueness.)

It's a good idea to examine other adverts or pick up leaflets of other practitioners/centres that are available in your locality. Then see how yours could be different from the others. If there are a lot of stress reduction practitioners then see if you can make yours different from the others. Perhaps you could change the size, typeface or headline of the advert or the look/style/colour of the leaflet to make it stand out.

Great Headlines

Your headline should be large, attractive, appeal to the reader, be active and should make the reader think 'this is for me'. The headline should contain the essence of your message. Headlines in tabloid newspapers can sometimes be read from 20 yards. So make it big. The success of your advert/leaflet can depend on the headline, so give it some thought. The best headlines stress the benefits:

5 Steps to Stop Smoking FOREVER!

Get Fit in Five Minutes a Day

You could try imparting news within the headline such as

New Discoveries in Learning

Famous Psychic Tells All

Generally anything with the word 'new' in it works well.

Short headlines can be made bigger and are therefore more effective, but long headlines work if they hit the mark

Find Out How To Tap into a £2 Million Market

Admittedly this is a long headline, but people are sure to read on just to find out what it's about.

Upper Case or Lower Case

You can use all upper case, all lower case or a mixture. Personally I prefer mixed case or all lower case. Lower case tends to look more informal and is easier to read than upper case. You could try different ways and ask other people for their comments.

Format

The headline does not have to be grammatically correct. You can get away with unorthodox phrases as long as the meaning is understood, that is what is important. Take a look at the headlines of newspapers and you will see what I mean.

Use Exciting Words

Use attention-grabbing words that sizzle with excitement, such as; amazing, discover, authentic, bargain, exclusive, fun, now, here, new, truth, urgent, yes, how to, you, your, win and special. If you don't have a Thesaurus, then it might be a good idea to invest in one.

Delete Extraneous Words

Get rid of the following words if possible: *is, are, that, which, were* etc. Tighten the headline up and make it punchy.

Finally, Be Honest and Clear

Does the headline tell what it's about? It should be clear, honest and accurate and convey the message simply and with gusto.

Use Graphics

Illustrations, photos, cartoons and any graphic serve to make your leaflet unique and grab the attention.

Photographs

A good photograph can work very effectively. The reader can see the practitioner and immediately make an emotional connection. It's easier to talk to someone on the phone if you have a face to connect it with, which can make it easy for that potential client to make that first important phone call. The photo also gives a lot of information to the reader which is of positive advantage. It also helps to give a lot of information about the practitioner, such as age, gender, friendliness etc., which they may be able to connect with at an emotional level. It might pay to ask a professional to take a photo of you which you can use in your leaflets. However, photos may not reproduce well if you are using cheaper paper.

If you practise one of the hundreds of body therapies, then it is almost essential that you have your photo on the leaflet. People want to know what the person is like before they let them put their hands on their body. They want to feel safe, and because you will initially be a stranger, if they know what you look like, you will be less of a stranger to them. You may even consider putting your photo on your business card.

Another way that body workers can use photos is to have the photo shot with the practitioner working on a client. The photo may allay fears by providing them with information, such as how much clothing is removed, does the consulting room have other people being worked on at the same time, etc.

Logo

If it's too costly (in terms of space) to include a photo in your advert, try using a logo instead. A logo is a graphic which sums up your business. It's best if the logo is black and white (line art) rather than having shades of grey. Line art is simple to recreate and is easier to handle for the printers of newspapers and magazines.

Designing a logo is quite specialised and it's worth it to have yours designed by a graphic designer. This is quite expensive; if you are lucky, you may know someone with artistic talents and knowledge of graphic design who will design one for you.

The use of a graphic can make or break your leaflet. A leaflet that is composed of nothing but text can look boring and unattractive. A graphic can spice up a dreary-looking leaflet. Keep your eyes open for other leaflets and see if and how they have used graphics. You may you need professional help from a designer to create a really effective leaflet. It may be expensive to have your leaflet professionally designed, but it can make such a difference and you can use his/her designs throughout your stationery and other leaflets you may produce in the future.

Colour

Coloured visuals usually look best, but are much more expensive and may not be worth the extra cost. Mono colour (usually black) on white is much cheaper.

The photograph you use must present the image of you that you want to portray. A passport photo in which you look like a criminal is obviously not an appropriate choice to use in a leaflet. Think of the image you wish to portray to others: authoritative, friendly, kind, technical, wise, approachable, sharp, enthusiastic, etc. and find the photo that best fits this image. Ask your friends and colleagues for their opinions on what message the public will see in your photo.

Getting a Response

Once you have written some copy for your ad, and have an idea of the layout, check it over for the AIDA Factor. AIDA stands for Attention, Interest, Desire and Action. Your advert should contain all of these elements.

Attention

Remember that your advert is competing with many other adverts and you must draw in the attention of the reader. As mentioned earlier, the commonest mistake is to put the name of the practitioner or centre at the top of the advert. As a headline this is not at all interesting to the reader. The headline should be catchy and immediately draw the attention of the reader.

THE THERAPY CENTRE

as a headline won't draw much attention whereas

STOP DEPRESSION NOW!

will. So it's important to choose the right headline.

Interest

Once you have got the attention of the reader with your headline, the next step is to arouse their interest. You can do this by amplifying and clarifying the headline and describing how your offer is of special interest to them. For example using the above headline 'Stop Depression Now' you could follow on with 'Do you wake up in the morning depressed? Do you feel like crying for no particular reason? Do you find it hard to cope with simple daily tasks? If the answer is Yes, then our new course for sufferers of depression can work wonders'.

Desire

You need to create in people an overwhelming need to have the service you offer. Make the readers say to themselves 'I want this'. The copy you write should be make the reader's mouth water with desire. Remember 'sell the sizzle, not the sausage'. How will it benefit or change them for the better if they have your treatment? Make it sound appealing and essential.

Action

Once the reader is interested and excited and ready to book a session, you must make it easy for them to make contact and inspire them to DO IT NOW!

An invitation to phone to make further enquiries is good. If possible offer them a reward for acting now, such as 'free introductory session if you phone before (date)'.

Your advert or leaflet should prompt the reader to action immediately. If it does not do this then the advert will be missed and the leaflet is likely to be left on one side and finally end up in the dustbin. The reader should be urged to take action there and then. So how can you do this?

The best way is to say it directly:

Call Now

Bring this flyer to our centre this week and get a 10% discount!

Send £30 deposit now!

Act Now!

Once Only Offer

REGISTER EARLY AND GET A FREE SESSION

You should make it easy for your potential clients to make contact with you. I have seen numerous adverts with no phone number, but which carry only an address. Presenting an obstacle such as this to your potential clients is disastrous. A phone number is essential and, if you can afford it, a free phone number can pay dividends.

After all your hard work of putting a leaflet together, it's no good if when your prospective client phones he/she gets an answer phone message, leaves a message, and then you don't get back to them for a week. Firstly, if you can't answer the phone, get another human to answer it for you. If that's not possible use an answer phone with an appropriate message. Then respond to their call as quickly as possible. Think of return calls as a necessary part of your business.

Monitor Which Adverts Work

Whenever you get a response (from anyone) ask how they heard about you. Keep a record of this. It is essential to know which adverts are working and how your clients find you. The benefits of keeping records is that you will know in future where to spend your precious money for the best results.

As a therapist, you will probably be using leaflets more than any other promotional method, so it is important that you are able to monitor what kind of response you get from each different distribution outlet. There are two ways of doing this: either ask your potential clients where they picked up your leaflet, or mark your leaflets in some distinguishable form for each location.

By marking your leaflets differently each time (insert a code in the text or change the colour/heading/date), you will know which leaflet the response is coming from. Since most of your responses come over the phone, your best bet is to use different colours of the paper for each batch of leaflets you print. When you get a response from a leaflet all you have to do is to ask the caller what colour the leaflet was.

If you are promoting a workshop, lecture or holiday and you have included an order form in your leaflet (or advert) then mark the order form in some way. You could do this by adding a prefix to the address (for instance, if you advertise in the Holistic London Guide then your address could be prefixed with 'Dept. HLG', or a less obvious code). Another way of marking leaflets is to 'scratch code' them. This works by including a series of letters or numbers in a nondescript place on the leaflet and getting the printer to scratch them off one by one as the leaflets are printing.

For example, let's say you are printing 12,000 leaflets and plan to distribute a third through the post, a third through local shops and cafes and a third as an insert in a magazine. Insert the numbers 1 2 3 in a reasonably visible place on your leaflet (such as the order form). Ask your printer to scratch one number off every 4000 leaflets. When the order form is sent in, you will know which method of distribution has just supplied you with a new client. Knowing which leaflets and which mode of distribution is working for you is essential, otherwise you can waste pots of money.

Creating a Great Leaflet

Writing Copy

You have four to catch the reader's attention with a leaflet, so it's important to make it strong. A common mistake in leaflet design is to put in too much text which can look boring. While it is important to explain what you do, you need to keep it brief.

Sum up what it is you offer, and the benefits of what you offer, in as few words as possible. The job of putting the words for a leaflet together is called copy writing, and there are professionals who do this for a living. Anyone who has ever put a leaflet together knows how much work and skill goes into it. You can do it yourself, though it's a good idea to ask other people to read and comment on it.

Know Your Audience

As I have stressed before, you should have a good idea of the type of person your are trying to reach: young/old, male/female, single/married, ethnic minorities, therapists, homeowners, rich/poor etc.

The overall impression you give in the leaflet needs to be geared to that market.

Testimonials

Having someone recommend you on your leaflet can work if you have not established yourself in the market and people don't know who you are. A testimonial is a genuine response from a former customer who states how pleased they are with your work. They need to be used with caution. Ones that don't work I think are those that are recommended by 'J. C. of Birmingham' (for example) - it looks as though the person is fictitious.

The testimonial should be from someone that the reader knows or can check up on. If your leaflet is distributed widely to members of the public then the testimonial should be from somebody well known, either generally or in the community. If the leaflet is aimed at a specialist market then the testimonial should be from somebody who is well known or reputable in the field. For example, if you are offering on-site massage to computer companies, then testimonials from other computer companies that have used your services will be very effective.

Qualifications and Credentials

Qualifications and credentials give you credibility. If you feel it's appropriate include your degree, postgraduate training and any other training or work which will help establish your credibility. But you are not limited to your academic prowess or training. Here are some other ideas: Author of..., Featured Speaker at..., Former College Lecturer, Founder of..., As seen on Channel...

The Overall Look

When you sit down to work out the overall look of the leaflet the first decision you will have to make is whether or not to fold the leaflet. If you decide it will be unfolded, you have to decide whether to have it vertical or horizontal. Vertical orientation (the technical word for which way up the paper goes) gives the appearance of alertness and action, while horizontal orientation tends towards calmness. Folding is more common and an A4 paper can be folded in two to give two A5 pages. Or you could go for two folds and have a thin upright leaflet. Try experimenting with some A4 sheets to see what you like best.

54

Something else to consider is having your leaflet double as a poster. If this is your intention, then obviously it should be printed on one side only. If you are publicising an event, you will want your leaflet to serve these two purposes, so remember when designing it that it is only one sided.

Bear in mind that the mode of distribution of your leaflet may dictate the shape of it. Think about how you are going to distribute your leaflet and where it is likely to go. If it's going to be left as a pile on a library table to be picked up by the public, then the library would like your leaflet to take up as little room as possible. They may object to displaying unfolded A4 sheets because they take up too much table space. You would be better off choosing a more discreet leaflet.

If your leaflets are likely to be displayed in racks, make sure that they fit. Not only do you not want them flopping all over the place, you will need the front page (or headline) to be visible. Many a time I have seen leaflets displayed in racks, with the headline completely hidden by the display.

The headline should be approximately one-third down the page to give maximum effect. Take a look at a number of books. The headline is not halfway down the page, but about a third from the top and in the centre. This is where your eye naturally falls on a page.

There are two lines of thought on the use of white space. Some designers prefer leaving lots of white space to accentuate the text, others prefer to cram the page with graphics and text. Lots of white space is easier on the eye, it appears less cluttered, and is easier to read. On the other hand, lots of text and graphics can give the appearance that there is lots happening.

Cut out your blocks of text and rearrange them onto the page to see how they look. If you have access to a photocopier you can enlarge or reduce parts and experiment with different layouts

Choosing the Right Typeface

There are thousands of different typefaces to choose from. A typeface can give a particular feel or flavour to a leaflet. If you do not know which typeface to choose then you can ask a typesetter or your local printer.

Typefaces can be either 'serif' or 'sans serif'. Serif typefaces have extra 'tails' on each character whereas the sans serif typefaces don't. Some typical serif typefaces are...Times, Palatino, Bookman.

Some typical sans serif typefaces are...Helvetica, Stone, Futura.

Sans serif are more often used for headlines as they tend to stand out. Serif typefaces are somewhat easier to read and are used more in blocks of text.

It's a good rule to use just one typeface on your leaflet, or perhaps two at the most. Beginners often make the mistake of using several and the results can look dreadful. It's probably best to choose a common typeface as this makes it easier for the reader to read. 'Times' is the most common typeface. It is very easy to read, and is very familiar. For variety and emphasis, you can vary the 'format' (bold, italic, underlined, etc.) and size of the typeface.

Colour and Paper Quality

You can use different coloured inks and different coloured paper. Combinations of these can be striking and make a huge difference to the look of your leaflet. Colour, however, costs money, so a trade-off is usually made between the use of colour and cost.

The cheapest paper to use is 80gsm (GSM stands for grams per square metre). Heavier (and lighter) paper costs more. Heavier paper increases the quality look and feel of the paper. Conqueror, which has a woven appearance is very attractive, but can be prohibitively costly.

The decision about whether to go for costly colour or heavier paper depends on the impression you want to give and also how many you are printing. If you are going for quantity, you will probably have to cut down on quality and vice versa. If you want to blanket your neighbourhood with leaflets, you will have to go for the cheapest paper; however, if you are promoting an expensive training and need to the leaflet to convey this, you may have to go for that glossy expensive look.

An acceptable intermediate choice is to go for black ink on coloured paper. You can get this reproduced in your local quick copy shop. Your local copy shop should have a range of coloured paper to choose from. The range of coloured paper goes from pastels, to fluorescent and vivid colours. Print out copies onto different coloured paper and see how they look from a distance. Eliminate those that do not stand out or don't work. Show this short-list to your friends and ask for their opinions.

From the collection of leaflets that you have picked up from your local library, shops etc. you should have a good idea of colours and which colour combinations work. Study them and don't be afraid to try different papers and inks.

Printing and Distributing

If you do not have a computer with a desktop publishing system, you will need to get your work typeset and any visuals 'scanned'. Your local quick copy shop may well be able to do this for you, so take your mock up to them and ask them to typeset it for you and to place any graphics.

Some printers also do typesetting and design. Once this is done, and before you get multiple copies printed, proof read it thoroughly! It's essential to make sure there are no mistakes before you go to the costly expense of getting it printed. It is not the printer's job to proof read it, so if there are any mistakes your precious leaflets may end up in the recycling bin. Pay particular attention to headlines and phone numbers. A mistake there could be disastrous and it's easier than you think to commit such a blunder.

Once your work has been typeset, then you will have a copy and will need to decide whether to get it copied at the shop or go to a printer. Generally printers do high-quality work, and it works out cheaper to use a printer depending on how many leaflets you want to print. Printers also use coloured inks. I tend to use a printer whenever possible as the quality of many quick print shops can be poor. However if you are printing a small number of leaflets (less than 300) a copy shop is more cost effective and it's easier to keep a check on the quality with a small print run. If you intend to print more than 500 leaflets you should consider using a printer rather than having them copied in a copy shop. Not only is a printer cheaper the more you get printed, but you have the choice of using more than one colour.

How Many Should You Print?

The amount of leaflets you want to print will depend on the response rate you expect to get. It can be very difficult to know what percentage of people will respond to your leaflet. Mail order companies work on getting a response rate of between one tenth of one percent to two percent.

The response rate depends of many factors: who gets it, how interesting it is, the timing, its visual appeal, etc. As a rule of thumb you could work on a response rate of 1% (one response in 100). However don't be surprised if the response rate is as little one per 1000 leaflets. If the response rate is low (much below 1%) then you will need to consider why. Was it a poor leaflet? Was it poorly targeted (i.e. did it reach your potential clients?) Was the timing right? It could just be that there is little demand for what you are doing.

Distribution

You can either place the leaflets at particular places in your local community, send them through the post, have them delivered door-to-door or insert them in a publication.

Placing leaflets in your local community can be effective. The leaflets need to be left at places where your potential clients are likely to congregate. Either you can find a distributor who offers this as a service (and there are not many who distribute to the right places) or do it yourself. It's quite easy to do it yourself if you have your own transport, and in many cases simply a push bike will do. Half the battle is knowing where these places are, so start by compiling a list of the places you already know about in your local community. Then ask friends and colleagues to add to this list. Pretty soon you will find the list will be sizeable enough to 'get your skates on' and hightail it round to these places. The good thing about doing it yourself is that you can make sure your leaflets are left in a prominent position and you can also meet the people in charge of these places and chat with them. They will often supply you with useful tips.

If your leaflet can be affixed to a wall or vertical surface, then you can pin it up on bulletin boards and walls. Do ask permission to do this first, unless there is a note saying that flyers can be put up.

Some typical places for distribution include; libraries, wholefood shops, wholefood restaurants, art galleries, independent cinemas, new age shops, essential oils shops, fitness centres, holistic health centres, medical surgeries, beauty parlours, car windshields, your own lectures, book shops and festivals (or any other relevant event; lectures, raves, etc.).

Less effective, but also worth thinking about are: supermarkets, launderettes, hospitals, hotel lobbies, colleges, restaurants, video shops, waiting rooms and restaurants.

If you are publicising an event you will need to get your leaflets out well before the event itself. If it's a local event then allow about two weeks, more for a workshop. Of course, as I have said before, the response rate depends on a number of factors.

Postal mailings or *direct mail* is very effective and you can be fairly sure the recipient of the leaflet will at least glance at it. It's expensive though. The trick is to have an effective mailing list. Either use your own - and you really should have assembled one by now - or 'rent' a list from someone. You need to find a mailing list that will reach the type of people that your leaflet is aimed at. The cost of direct mail is about £300 per thousand (which includes the cost of stamps). One way of reducing the expense is to find another practitioner who will share the cost of a mailout. You could also ask a business to place your leaflets in their mailout this is called cooperative mailing). They will charge you for this service, but it will not be nearly as expensive as renting a list and direct mailing yourself.

Door-to-door mailing (putting leaflets through letter boxes by hand) provides cheap and local coverage if you do it yourself. However, the effectiveness of this method depends on whether the people in your local community will be interested in what you are offering. If you receive a local paper through your door then it's likely that they also distribute leaflets as a sideline. Simply phone them up and ask if they take inserts.

There are also companies that provide this service. A list of these can be found in the *Yellow Pages* under 'Circular & Sample Distributors'. Distributors can offer some degree of targeting. For example they can distribute to home owners, or to houses priced above a certain value, or to houses where the occupiers have a certain minimum income, as well as many other types. They charge approximately £15 per thousand leaflets, which is cheap. However, the response rates are not likely to be high – which means that you need to send out a larger number of leaflets this way.

Another method is to place your leaflet in a publication. Your leaflet is then called an 'insert'. This can be cost effective, but it must be the right publication. The publication must be distributed locally (if your service is local) and must be the right kind of publication. The fee charged can vary from £15 to £150 per thousand, so it's worth shopping around.

Advertising in Publications

There are two things to remember when buying advertising space in a newspaper or magazine; advertise to the right audience and advertise locally!

Advertise to the Right Audience

It's obviously best to advertise your services to those people who are interested in what you have to offer. So finding the right medium to advertise in is important. When you are considering taking out an ad in a paper, find out who reads it. One way to do this is to ask for a media pack from the newspaper in question. Most magazines or papers will have done a reader survey and will be able to tell you the kind of people that will read the publication.

Advertise Locally

The biggest mistake that practitioners make when they first start buying advertising is that they advertise in national magazines. Even if the magazine they choose is specialised, it's unlikely that anyone in Scotland is going to come all the way to London for an aromatherapy session.

There are about eighty specialist magazines in the holistic field in the UK, but very few of them serve the local community. However, if you can find a holistic magazine that serves say, Birmingham, and you happen live there, then obviously this is the best place to advertise.

Other local publications include the Yellow Pages and Thompsons Directory. Both of these are good places to advertise. They are expensive, but should produce results because they serve the local community. If you practice in London, Brainwave publishes *The Holistic London Guide*. This is an ideal place to advertise because it is distributed in London only, it reaches people who are interested in alternative therapies, and it's printed in high volume.

Advertising locally is important, but if you are selling a product, or if you think the public will travel long distance for the service you are offering, then you should consider advertising outside your local community.

There are a vast number of publications you can advertise in and you may be at a loss to know where to begin. It's more cost effective in this case to promote yourself in specialist publications. For instance if you are a counsellor, then think about which specialist publications your potential clients are likely to read.

Using The Media

Getting Your Name in the Papers

Getting Editorial in Newspapers and Magazines

The most appealing thing about getting an article or editorial in a newspaper or magazine is that it's free. It's also gratifying to see your name in the papers. However it will cost you time, thought and luck. The other great thing is that readers will believe an article they read, much more than an advert. It's not too difficult to get editorial in small circulation publications because they often run on a tight budget and don't have many (if any) paid writers. It is, however, much more difficult to get editorial in the national papers and magazines. Advertising, in comparison to getting editorial, is promoting yourself the lazy way. With an advert you simply buy space in a publication, write your copy and send a cheque and it's more or less guaranteed a home will be found for your advert. Getting an article or news item published needs wits and some degree of talent.

Getting Editorial in the Specialist Publications

Many of the small specialist publications are only too happy to have an article appear through their letter box which is tailor made for their publication. You may already be fairly familiar with these publications and may even subscribe to them.

Press Releases

The most common way of connecting (and of getting an interview if you want one) with the media is through a press release. Many PR people spend a lot of their time writing press releases and other material that is intended for the press.

A press release should be a simple document that briefly and effectively communicates a message (a single A4 page is the ideal length). Since newspapers really can't afford to employ an army of reporters to cover every single event, the press rely to some extent an people sending them information in the form of press releases. However, keep in mind that most newspapers (except the smallest of the local papers) receive hundreds of press releases every week and that only one in ten actually makes it into print. For the major regional and national newspapers this figure is even lower.

Don't let this prevent you from sending in a press release! You just need to make sure that your story has that special appeal which makes it stand head and shoulders above the rest.

Some of the main reasons that press releases don't make it into print are as follows:

1. No news

Either the press release does not contain any news, the news is insignificant, or it's too specialised. In a word, it's boring.

2. Not targeted at the right publication

Many press releases cover too broad a range of information. When writing your press release, keep the publication you are sending it to in mind. If you are sending out a blanket of releases, try to separate the newspapers and magazines into various groups (i.e. local, national, health and spiritual) and write a separate press release for each group.

3. Badly written

This is the most common reason that a press release will not get into the paper: the news is too deeply buried and the press release is full of technical jargon. You need to make sure that the press release states its purpose in the first paragraph, that it is written clearly and that it reads like a news item.

What Your Press Release Should Look Like

Although you are perfectly free to style the press release in any way that you want, certain stylistic norms should be followed:

Layout:

• typed (not hand written) and double spaced;

- it should fit on a single A4 page (if you must use more than one page, then write 'more' or 'continued' at the bottom of the first page);
- the margins should be as follows: two inches at the top and one and a half inches left and right (this leaves space for editor's notes);
- don't use your own letterhead or business paper for the press release;
- include a release date (that is, the date of the issue of the publication you want your information printed in);
- at the end of the press release, write 'End'. The editor will know that whatever you write after this is intended for their eyes only. These addendum should include a contact name, daytime telephone number and out-of-office hours telephone number.

As far as content is concerned, your press release should, above all, be interesting and newsworthy. Again, there are some conventions that may help you to write a more effective press release.

A successful press release should have:

- **A Good Headline**

  If the headline doesn't grab someone's attention in the first four seconds, you've lost your audience. So you need a good headline. First of all, don't use too many words, six is a maximum. Spend some time thinking of a really effective headline, something that grabs the attention, a play on words, something that is gutsy and packs a punch. Of course, ideally the headline should encapsulate the article. So write your article before you come up with that snappy, attention grabbing headline;

- **A Short Snappy First Paragraph**

  All the main facts should be included (who, what, why, when, where) in one or two sentences.

- **Short Paragraphs.**

  Three sentences maximum per paragraph.

- **Important Details Included**

  These include dates, names, times, location, your number, etc. and which should be checked for accuracy before you send your press release off.

- **A Brief Statement about Yourself**

This is especially important if you or your organisation are not well known.

- **No Superlatives**
  Words such as best and first should be avoided, as well as overstated adjectives (marvellous, brilliant, excellent) and phrases (announces, is pleased to announce that...).
- **No Jargon**
  Jargon tends to marginalise your audience, so avoid it, especially if it is going to the general press.

Including a good photograph in your press release can make a great impression, however, don't forget to caption it. If you are formatting your press release on a computer and have your photograph on disk, you might want to state in the addendum (the part of the press release that is intended for the editor's eyes only) that you have a copy of the photo on disk. If they want to see it, they can contact you.

If your intention in sending out the press release is to get a journalist to write a story on you, don't be too impatient, it may take some time before they contact you.

If you don't want the story to break too early then use an 'embargo' on your press release. At the top of the press release, type 'EMBARGO: Not for Publication Before (date and/or hour)'.

Don't hesitate to write up different versions of the press release to go to different publications.

Distributing the press release

You can either fax or post the press release. If you can, address the press release to a person, rather than a job title. Often you will find a list of all of the employees and their titles in the first few pages of a magazine or newspaper, or you may want to call them up and ask who you should address your press release to. It may be that you will need to send a press release to three different sections of one newspaper. If this is the case, send off three press releases, it will increase your chances of getting your name in the paper. Do not just address your press release to the publication, with no name or job title.

To find a list of publications try *The Writer's and Artist's Yearbook*. This is quite cheap and widely available. You could also try *The PR Planner*, *Willen's Press Guide* or *Brad*, although the latter is more useful if you are planning a large advertising campaign since it gives information about advertising and advertising contacts.

As well as having to write up different press releases for different types of publications, you will need to check the release dates of the various publications. You will probably be mailing to daily publications, weeklies, monthlies and quarterlies, so make sure that you allow enough lead time for the less frequently published ones. Quarterlies will need your press release six months in advance, two to three months for weeklies and monthlies, four weeks for dailies.

If you want to send your information to other media, such as television and radio, then you it's called a 'news release', although it may be almost identical to your press release.

When Journalists Contact You

Most features for a publication will be written either in-house or by a freelance journalist. If a journalist wants to write up a story based on your press release, they will most likely phone you up and ask for an interview. Whatever happens, you should be prepared, and have the relevant information near the phone for at least a couple of months after you have sent out your press release.

When a journalist does contact you, make sure that you allow plenty of time for the interview itself. If they say it will only take half an hour, give yourself an hour. You never know how well it will go; maybe you will captivate them so much that they will stay talking with you for quite some time. Although this is not a likely scenario, you really don't want to have to kick the journalist out of your home because you have a client coming in five minutes - it wouldn't make for good copy.

When contacted by a journalist, try to have all the information you need at hand. If you don't, try to get back to them as soon as you can. Remember, having an article about yourself printed has ten times the impact as an ad in the same publication would have. Besides, it's free! As much as you can, try to respect the wishes of the journalist when it comes to scheduling a time for the interview. Again, during the interview, try not to use too much jargon. Use accessible language whenever you can, and explain any specialised terms that you want used in the article.

If you can't supply the information that they want, or do the interview within the time required by the journalist, then admit this, so that goodwill is maintained between you. If they require facts, figures or photos, have them ready and waiting at the time of the interview and in a format that the journalist can use (if they need photocopies or a copy of something on disk for example).

It's not a good idea to ask to see an article before it goes to print, since this may offend. You could make an offer to check facts and be available to answer any queries. If you are asked to do this, comment only on the facts and information and not on the particular style of the article.

Kinds of publication

Holistic Press

There are just under a hundred 'holistic' magazines in the UK. Their circulation is relatively small, but because their market is so specialised, it's worth targeting them for most of your press releases. Most of these publications are in magazine format and they are often subscriber based and therefore not readily available in newsagents. The non subscription magazines can often be found in specialised bookstores or health food shops.

General Press

General press refers to all publications which are not aimed at one particular audience. There are over 2,000 newspapers in the UK. These include regional, national, local and perhaps some more specialised publications. The general press, because they are general, carry specialist articles about many things at different times. Many of the bigger papers have a separate section on health, or health and beauty.

For material to be accepted by the general press, the editors need to be certain that the news item will be of interest to a significant portion of their readers. In the case of holistic practitioners and centres, it's unlikely that your news item would be of interest to enough of their readers. For this reason, targeting the general press is not such a good idea, unless you think that you have a really hot news item or something that you can get into one of their specialist sections.

Local Press

Local newspapers are worth targeting because they are distributed locally and, ideally, most of your clients should be recruited from your area. Also, because these local papers have a very small staff, and don't have the budget to do extensive reporting, it is likely that you could get your own editorial printed.

Local papers generally appear weekly, although there are exceptions to this rule. For financial reasons, these papers are often syndicated, or published in a series, so that the same editorial or article will appear in two towns simultaneously even though the names of the papers are different.

Local newspapers can be divided into two groups, the ones that cost money and the ones that are free. The ones that cost money contain up to 50% editorial copy, whereas the freebies contain about 10% editorial (in some cases even less) and 90% advertising (or more). Quite often the freebies only have a staff of one or two people.

The local papers tend to rely greatly on a network of contributors who are often unpaid and who provide local interest news or specialised articles. Because the staffing levels are so low, if you present a press release and a well-written editorial, you may find that it is printed with very few changes to it. Keep this in mind when sending a press release to smaller papers, make sure that anything you send to them is ready to be printed verbatim.

Consumer Publications

Consumer magazines tend to be national and can be considered part of the national press. Most of these consumer magazines are women's interest magazines and publish at least one issue a year related to health. It may be worth contacting these publications if you think that reaching a broad national audience would benefit your practice. However, many of their 'feature articles' are actually paid advertisements, or the articles might contain information about one of the products that are advertised in the magazine. Find out about this before you start blindly mailing out press releases to what may turn out to be a glorified brochure.

Listings Magazines

Listings magazines are worth targeting because they tend to be local. Usually you can only find these in big cities, since local leisure and community activities in rural areas are generally covered by the local press. If you do live in a large city, it's worth collecting as many listings magazines as you can get your hands on. Find out if they advertise workshops or courses for free, many do and if this is the case, you have nothing to lose by sending in the details of an upcoming event at your practice.

(Sample Press Release)

Release Date: Monday, March 3, 1997

Do You Want a Smack?!

Samuel Jay believes that when parents hit their children they are unwittingly replicating what their parents did to them. He is holding a one day workshop on the 29th of March at **The Communication Centre** aimed at parents who want to find effective ways of disciplining their children without recourse to violence.

The theme of the one-day workshop will be on how parents handle their children at the supermarket. According to Samuel, this is the most likely place for children to be threatened or hit in public.

He will be using role playing, and role reversal, as a starting point to the day's activities. Parents will be encouraged to take part in this role playing, since it provides such an effective way of communicating emotions, but people who do not want to participate are welcome to watch.

An established therapist of 30 years, Samuel will be provide a supportive and safe environment in which participants can relate their own childhood experiences of discipline. The participants will then be invited to offer their opinions on effective and ineffective methods of child discipline. There will also be a discussion on what discipline means to the various participants and some of the reasons that it is used. As well as facilitating participant discussions, Samuel will be presenting many of the techniques outlined in his book 'Effective Parenting in the Information Age'.

The workshop will be held at The Communication Centre, Nightingale Lane, South Clapham, SW9 from 10am until 6pm

Couples are encouraged to attend together. There will be a day-care centre, run by a qualified child care worker, open during the length of the workshop.

Tickets for the workshop and for day-care are available by calling Samuel Jay on (0181) 627 0954.   **End**

Contact Name: Samuel Jay

Daytime Telephone Number: 0181 627 0954

Out of Office Hours: 0181 897 4538

How to Get on the Radio

Radio is a unique means of communication. Many people listen to the radio throughout their day or evening, be they at home, in the car or at work. They can continue to do other things while they listen - unlike television or newspapers and magazines which demand their full attention. Spending some time listening to the radio yourself and becoming familiar with the programmes and presenters is a good way of finding out which programmes are most suitable for you. As a radio interview will reach a great number of people, its worth doing a bit of research so you can promote yourself effectively on the right programme.

If you want to reach a broad range of people, radio is an ideal way of promoting yourself. If you enjoy and are good at talking about what you do and don't feel intimidated by large audiences then a radio interview is an exciting challenge.

Decide on Your Message

Decide what message you want to put across to the listeners. What do you want to say about yourself and your work? Then you can decide when is the best time to be on air to get your message across to people who will be interested.

The next thing to do is to listen to the programme you want to appear on. Get an idea of how the programme is presented, of it's style and format. Listen to other interviews and how people come across on the radio. By doing this bit of 'research' you can get an idea of what works and what doesn't .

It's hard to believe, but there really are people who have turned up for interviews with no idea of the programme they are about to broadcast on. They had not done any preparatory work to find out what they needed to know about the programme and the interview. A little bit of preparation before the interview will allow you to relax, feel comfortable and enjoy yourself.

Get Your Message Across

There are different options involved in doing a radio interview. It does not necessarily involve going live on national radio which may well terrify the faint hearted! If you're not nervous about public speaking then go for it ! But there are ways of easing yourself into the world of radio.

Appearing on hospital radio is one way of having an easier first experience. Many hospitals do have their own radio station. Contact your local hospital to find out if they do. They should be able to point you in the right direction if they don't.

If you like more of a challenge, your local radio station will be the place for you to begin. Phone the sales department, say you are interested in advertising with them and ask for more information. They will probably send you details of their rates and a media pack that includes information about programme policy, the physical transmission area and a profile of the listeners.

To Go Live or Not

There are three choices to consider, depending on how confident you feel about appearing on the radio. You may have nerves of steel and no hesitations about doing an interview live. If this is the case, then make sure you are well prepared and enjoy yourself. Once you've done it the first time it will get easier and easier.

A second option is to do a pre-recorded programme. This means that your interview is recorded first and gives the editor a chance to correct anything they are not happy with. If you find you are hesitating, or don't like the way you answered a question, you can do it again and the first version will be edited. This takes a lot of pressure off the interview and makes it easier to relax and come across in a clear, confident manner. The only drawback is that often the editing can be dramatic. For example, when the final broadcast edition is less than two minutes long when you thought it was going to be at least ten!

The third choice is to do an interview on a late night show. Although you will reach fewer listeners in the night, you will probably be able to do a longer interview. This is a good option if you can stay alert at midnight and don't mind having a smaller audience.

Be Prepared

It is important to ask some questions before the interview so you know what is about to happen.

Find out if the interview is live or pre-recorded. If it's live, how much time do you have? If it's pre-recorded how long will the final edited version of the interview be? Ask who will be interviewing you and whether or not you will be interviewed alone. If there will be other people interviewed with you, find out who they are.

It is important to make sure that the programme's style and audience suit you. What sort of programme would you prefer to appear on? Are you a light-hearted 'easy listening' sort of speaker or are you a more serious talker? Make sure you will fit in and feel at ease with the programme's style.

If the programme allows the public to 'phone-in' and ask questions, you need to be prepared to answer anything. Try to do as much preparatory work as possible; only the most inane or insane questions should stump you. You could practise answering unexpected questions with a friend before the interview. While 'on air', use a pen and paper to write down the caller's name so you can address them when answering the question. Finally, try to find out in what context the interview is going to be used.

Appearing on Television

It could happen to you! It's easier than you think to make an appearance on television. Take a look at how many television stations there are. Each of these stations has to fill hours and hours of airtime and spend as little as possible.

Granted, it *is* quite hard to get an interview on nationwide broadcast television, but getting onto cable and satellite programmes is really not that difficult if you have an interesting enough story to tell. (Advertising, however, is prohibitively expensive - about a quarter of a million pounds for a 30 second commercial. However, commercial time on local cable stations may be within the bounds of larger centres. The question is, would the response be worth the cost?)

Most larger cities have at least a few cable television stations which carry local-interest programmes and a lot of satellite channels have 24hour coverage, which means they have a lot of low-budget air time (that is, air time which does not attract much advertising money) that needs filling. If you can come up with something interesting and colourful enough, you could experience your own '15 seconds of fame'.

So don't be intimidated, don't leave television appearances strictly to actors, politicians and so called *experts*. Television presents an unparalleled opportunity to reach a vast audience; if you think you have a great *scoop*, you should seriously consider a television appearance.

Like so many other forms of media, television provides an opportunity to shamelessly promote yourself for free (unless you decide to advertise, which is probably too prohibitively expensive for your budget). One thing that television provides which no other media outlet can is the opportunity to demonstrate the product or service that you are offering.

One of the problems with appearing on television is that you almost always have to wait to be asked. However, the only way you'll be ever be asked is if you let them know that you are available. Send your press releases, press clippings and brochures to the local stations on a regular basis; get to know someone who works there; make some contacts. Most people who appear on these specialised local interest shows are *friends of a friend*. In other words, they are there because someone involved with the show has already heard of them, not because they were specially sought out.

Why Would They Ask Me?

Let us set up a hypothetical scenario. You have been regularly (say, quarterly), sending press releases to your local television station. The lastest press release even contained a cutting of an article you wrote for a regional paper. Because of these regular mailings, the staff at the local station know about you and consider you to be the local 'past lives' expert.

A television journalist from this station rings you up for information. He want to know if you know anyone who might appear on the station's midday health show.

You have seen the show before; it is documentary-style, with a slightly over the top tabloid slant, but nevertheless quite informative. The next instalment is to be entitled 'The Unconscious Mind'. Because of your constant self-promotion, you were naturally one of the first people they rang up.

While talking with the journalist, you impress her with your knowledge of health issues and she invites you to appear on the show as an 'expert' in past life therapy.

This is your big chance! The first thing to consider is whether or not you are comfortable with being considered an *expert* in past life therapy. If you don't want to appear as an *authority*, you may want to offer a demonstration of your therapy instead. This is, after all, more visually appealing and entertaining than simply talking about what you do.

It's worth talking to the journalist more to discuss these details. If you are a bona fide 'authority' (i.e. you have written articles, given talks and/or run training courses) then fine, flaunt it! It is, however, inadvisable to advertise yourself as an expert if you are not considered one by at least a few of your contemporaries.

Let's look at another scenario. You are asked if you would like to appear on a local news show to defend your therapy. A local woman (not one of your clients) has had past life therapy and claims that she now has such extreme nightmares that she is unable to sleep, and that it is affecting her work, her social life and her appetite. In short, past life therapy has ruined her life. (This is just an example, hopefully nothing as extreme will ever happen to you.)

You know that she is going to appear on the television damning your therapy in front of a large audience. You now have two options: either ignore the whole fiasco and hope that very few people see the show, *or* appear on the show to defend the honour of your chosen profession. If you've got the guts and have had some previous television or radio experience, you should consider it. Why? It's great publicity for you. You will be seen by these viewers as an expert. It's not you that has been accused of making false promises. You are simply there to represent your profession. Besides, how many invitations to appear on television do you expect to get in your lifetime?

These are two possible scenarios for appearing on television. Another is that you will have somehow been able to interest a network in doing special feature solely on you and your therapy. If you can manage it, this would be quite a coup, but to get to that point you would need to work hard to make the necessary contacts.

The trick with television, as with radio, is to be prepared and well armed. Know what you want to say, and think about what the interviewer is likely to ask. The presenter wants a lively, colourful and entertaining program. If you have nothing to say and are not ready for the questions, you will appear dull, lifeless, and maybe even a little stupid. So you need to have a message, and to present this message in a lively and entertaining way. Be colourful, that is, as colourful as you are comfortable being.

If you work with groups or run workshops then you are probably quite an effective public speaker. There's no reason why you should be overwhelmingly anxious about appearing on television, after all, you speak to the public every day. It's natural that you'll be a little nervous and self conscious, but the more prepared you are, the less nervous you will be.

When Opportunity Knocks

Preparation is essential if you are going to get the interview to go your way. If you haven't thought about what you want to say, then the interviewer will have total control. If she feels a need to liven up the interview, you may find yourself faced with some stimulating questions which you aren't prepared to answer.

The first radio interview I ever did, was about a book I had co-written called *Survivor's London*. There were three of us being interviewed and the first question we were asked was "This book is about alternative lifestyles and alternative living - so what exactly *is* alternative?".

A pretty obvious question, but all three of us were thrown and didn't know how to respond to this question. We fumbled badly. Each of us in turn came up with an inane response before passing the question on. By the time we had all spoken, we'd come up with a passable but fantastically long-winded and unfocused response. It was just lucky that there were three of us there to share the burden

The interview proceeded to go from bad to worse; the fiasco of that very first question had embarrassed and distressed us. It wasn't that the interviewer was antagonistic, but that we weren't prepared to steer the interview, we didn't have any specific points to make.

When the interviewer opened the book at random, it happened to fall open on the page about living with disabilities in London. She asked us a question about that particular entry and again we didn't quite know what to say. Because it was a phone-in show, people started calling in about the problems of being a disabled person in London. The interview became a forum on living with disabilities! While this may have been a worthwhile discussion, it didn't accurately represent the wide range of issues covered in the book.

We left that interview with the feeling that we had just wasted one of the biggest promotional opportunities of our lives. We had expected the experience to go much more smoothly, although we had only been dimly aware of what we had wanted to say. Our objective had been to promote the book, and we had failed to grasp the opportunity.

Get Three points across

One of the best tips I can give you for taking charge of the direction your interview takes is to have three major points you want to get across. More than three points and you may very well confuse the audience. Less than three and you won't have anything to fall back on, and will probably run out of things to say.

Take time to develop these three separate ideas as if they were going to be all you will talk about; make them interesting, dynamic; prepare an amusing anecdote or example; and prepare a way of connecting these three main ideas.

Using the example of the past life therapy interview, let's establish our message in three main points. You have been asked to appear on a program entitled 'The Unconscious Mind' as an *expert* on past life therapy. The producer is aiming to get your views on reincarnation, religion, karma and so on.

From your perspective as a past life therapist, this show is going to be a forum for advertising your practice and getting some free publicity. There are hundreds of things you could say about your therapy in relation to the topics that are going to be covered, but you need to narrow it down to three main ideas if you want to make a strong impression.

You decide that you are going to discuss the following points:

A. Past life therapy works. This is going to be the first point you bring up, in response to the question on reincarnation (as in, "I have no proof of reincarnation, but I do have proof that past life therapy works).

B. Past life therapy works best for people who suffer from anxiety. You plan to bring up this point in response to a question on karma.

C. Only trained, knowledgeable, and preferably experienced, practitioners are effective.

For each of these points you are going to have a very brief 'speech' prepared, with examples and explanations, and you are going to rehearse and re-rehearse until you can get each point across in as little time as possible.

Getting Your Message Across

It's great if you have established what you want to say - now you need to say it. You are going to have plenty of opportunity for this, but it may not be as easy as you think. Consider each question in the interview as an opportunity to get your message across. But you don't want to get just any message across, you want to state your predetermined points, right? So you need to establish a link between each question and your message, somehow incorporating your points into your answers. This is an art, but it's one that most of us practice all the time (politicians are especially adept at it).

Using our past life therapy example, let's say that you want to state that past life therapy works especially well for people who suffer from anxiety.

Question: Are you a vegetarian?

Answer: Yes, I am. I strongly believe that if we treat our bodies properly, then our bodies will be able to correct our emotional imbalances without therapy, to a certain extent. However, some people, especially very anxious or nervous people, find that even though they eat a healthy diet, and live an active lifestyle, they still carry around a lot of unaccounted for anxiety or tension. This kind of anxiety is often old and deep rooted and I find that these are the kind of people who benefit the most from my past life therapy.

You are not there to answer the interviewer's questions, but to get your message across, so don't be shy about linking up seemingly unrelated topics. Everyone does it.

It is important that you keep the message as simple as you can. This will make it much easier to link topics, but it will also prevent you from going into detail about an obscure point. You know everything there is to know about your therapy, and could probably talk about it for hours, but television is not the place to do this.

Remember who your audience are. They may be eating their dinner, cleaning, minding their kids, ironing, and more than likely are paying scant attention to the programme. You need to keep your message as snappy, colourful and entertaining as possible. Remember, too, that on television there is no harm in repeating yourself in order to get your main points across.

Find Out More

Before you decide what your chosen message is going to be, find out certain things about the show.

- Why have they chosen you to come and do this particular interview?
- What would you say the 'style' of the program is?
- Given this 'style', what kind of questions do you think are going to be asked?
- How much does the interviewer already know about your therapy?
- Where is she getting this information from?
- Can you see this source, article, book, etc., before you go for the interview?
- What does the interviewer want to learn about your therapy from the interview?
- How long does she expect you to be on the show?
- Will the interview be live or recorded?
- Are there going to be other people being interviewed?

When it is time to appear on the show, bear the following in mind

- The interviewer will have a list of questions to ask you, but won't necessarily stick to this preset script if a more interesting line comes up during the interview.
- These preset questions are often not formulated until quite close to the time of filming, but the interviewer generally has some idea of what kind of questions they are likely to ask you. It is worthwhile trying to find out what these are likely to be. A little while before you go on the air, ask what the first question is going to be - it is common courtesy for the interviewer to let you know.

- An interview is a way of delivering a message, whether this message is your own or the interviewer's *is up to you*. Go to the interview with something to say.

What Are Some Likely Questions?

It is impossible to know exactly what you are going to be asked, but it doesn't take a psychic to figure out what you are likely to be asked. Generally, a program is either *positive* or *negative*.

You are going to appear on a *positive* show, the questions are more likely to be ones that will tease out more about the therapy itself. They are looking for good, colourful, lively news.

If, however, the program is a *negative* one, they will be aiming to portray you or your therapy in a negative light, particularly in an investigative, journalistic type interview. The questions are likely to be probing and hard-edged.

In either case, remember that you are there not to answer the interviewer's questions, but to get your own points across. If possible, watch the program beforehand on television. Watch out for the kind of questions that are asked. Is it an analytical program? Do they seek to uncover or do they seek to inform? You can find this out just by listening to what kind of questions are asked. Put yourself into the interviewees' shoes; how did this person get on the show, what do their main points seem to be, if they have any. Do you think it was a successful appearance for the interviewee? Once you have an idea of some of the questions that you are likely to be asked, use them in your role play.

Create a Picture

It's possible to make an impact on the audience by creating a picture in their minds and offering a story line. People love stories and pictures, anything that helps them to understand a concept. Which do you think is the more vital, interesting statement?

Osteopathy can help with a wide range of different ailments, including bad posture and back sprains.

One of my clients, a trainer of racing horses, sprained her back and for three weeks didn't leave her bed. She came to see me using crutches and I could see that the effort cost her

considerable pain. After our hour long session, she rushed out to go to an important appointment... and left her crutches in my office!

Besides being obviously more interesting, the second statement is told first-hand and tells the audience quite a bit about osteopathy without going into what can seem as boring detail.

Which of the following two examples has the more impact?

Our past life therapy centre has over 8 000 square feet.

In order to be effective, past life therapy requires a special atmosphere. Our three large, beautiful practising rooms have been specially decorated with all natural material and textiles to be calm, light and spacious.

The first statement is actually a non statement, it means nothing. It is almost impossible for anybody other than an estate agent to visualise how much space 8,000 square feet is. The second statement, although it is a bit longer, is much more emotive and evocative.

Role Play

After you have found out what the show is about and have written a 'script' of sorts for yourself, it's worth taking some time to rehearse it. Invite some friends and co-workers to do some role playing. Practice various ways of getting your three points across.

It's one thing to be clear in your head about what you want to say, but it's another thing to actually say it. Role play is a great way to practise incorporating your message into the interview and will give you added confidence about your impending television appearance.

Playing The Game

You may think that all that has been said about radio and television interviews sounds like *playing a game*. You may feel media world of sound bytes and visual bytes that we live in is *phoney*. Perhaps it is. If so, you then need to decide whether you want to appear in the media at all, but if you do, then you will need to be familiar with the tools and systems of the media to get your message across. Fortunately you don't need to become a total media person who lives and breathes the world of snappy images and sounds.

A Few Words of Advice

The normal rules of conversation do not apply in a television interview, or any interview for that matter. It's not your job to be the interviewer's friend. You are there to get your message across and for no other reason.

- Don't get too cosy, this can make you look either sloppy or just plain ludicrous, depending on the style of the show. Sit up straight, maintain eye contact with the interviewer, *be calm and professional*.

- Don't let yourself be interrupted. In normal conversation you would probably stop speaking if someone interrupted you, but on television these rules of etiquette don't apply. If the interviewer cuts in on what you are saying, *raise your voice slightly and finish your point*.

- Don't be shy about pointing out an unfair or untrue statement. You may be accustomed to ignoring the occasional cheap shot, after all if you know it's not true, no harm done, right? Not on television. The audience doesn't necessarily know what is true and what is not, it's up to you to let them know. This can be tricky, because you don't want to seem to be on the defensive. The best method is to somehow *link* the unfairness or untruthfulness of the statement into your response.

- I've already said it, but it's an important point: if you feel that you are being attacked, *don't get defensive*. Instead, calmly refute the statement. Don't get visibly angry.

- When you are speaking, be assertive. Don't say 'in my opinion', or 'in my experience', just *say what you are going to say with confidence*. You probably know much more about what you are talking about than the interviewer does, so make sure the audience knows it.

- Remember who your audience is. Don't bore them, don't go into great detail and above all, *don't use jargon*.

- Finally, remember that every opportunity that you get to speak is an opportunity to relay your message to the audience - *make the most of it!*

Ideas For Self Promotion

Getting the Most Out of Festivals

Exhibiting

Renting a stall at local exhibitions is a good way to get yourself known, concentrate your mind, meet the public and make contacts with potential associates. At these events you will get an opportunity to meet other people and get direct feedback from them - what they like about your therapy and what their resistances to it are. If something seems to invite a particularly enthusiastic response, find out what it is in particular that is so appealing. You may discover that there are hidden benefits of your therapy that you weren't previously aware of. If you discover a certain type of people who seem particularly interested in your therapy, you can start targeting them more effectively in your marketing.

You will be able to try out new techniques in the way you practise your therapy and see how the public responds.

You will have a chance to practise your selling technique. You will be able to see how other people market themselves, and gain some inspiration from their literature, brochures and pamphlets.

The main benefit of taking part in exhibitions is to make new contacts with prospective clients. This face to face contact is very important. Once a potential client has had some contact with you, and feels like they know you, they are much more likely to take the all important step of coming to see you.

Once again let me remind you not to forget to get their details; their name, address and telephone number. There is no harm in asking if they would like to book an appointment or an initial consultation there and then. Have your appointment book ready just in case. You could also offer to give them a ring after the show, or to put them on your mailing list. Essentially you are there to sell your service and recruit as many clients as you can.

One way of promoting your therapy at the show is to sell short therapy sessions at the show. Of course, some therapies lend themselves to this much more easily than others. Tarot, massage, aromatherapy and reflexology are all quite popular with the public at shows, and you will find that you can at least recoup the cost of the stand. Of course, if you can't actually sell your therapy, try giving a demonstration. If you practice a therapy such as yoga or tai chi, giving a demonstration at a show is a very easy way to promote your therapy to large crowd of people. Not only that, but your potential clients will get a very clear idea of what your therapy involves.

One of the things about participating in shows is that it will focus your mind and give you a clear deadline, something in the near future to plan for and look forward to. Of course, the more time and effort you put into planning and promoting your attendance, the more you will get out of the show. You could, for example, use your mailing list to mail out details of the event and let people know that you will be there. Maybe some of the people on your mailing list have yet to meet you in person. Some people are, understandably, wary of initiating therapy with someone who they have yet to meet face to face and you are presenting a perfect opportunity to gain people's trust.

Another way of promoting your participation in the show is to send out a press release. If you do this, then make sure that your press release contains all the essential information: your name, your practice, the name of the festival, when and where it is taking place, how much it costs, how long the festival has been running, exactly what you will be doing there, and any other pertinent information. Also, try to make it as interesting and eye-catching as possible. You could include a picture of yourself practising your therapy, or of your centre if it is in a particularly beautiful spot - anything that is attractive and relevant to what you do.

You could also write an interesting editorial about what you do, including details of your up-and-coming appearance in the festival.

If the media does make it to the show, you could make some really useful media contacts that you can use in the future to promote yourself.

It's *essential* to have a business card and some leaflets and brochures on display on a rented stall at the show, which you could hand out to any interested parties. Also, get as many cards and brochures from the other exhibitors as this will increase your database and possibly provide you with some useful contacts for the future.

Sell It

In addition to the points covered in this book under the section on 'selling', there are some other things you need to bear in mind when you are selling face to face.

Before you go to the festival, you need to clarify in your own mind what is unique about what you offer, what are the benefits of what you do. It's worthwhile getting quite passionate about what you offer. The most effective ways of selling a product or service in person is to be passionate, excited and enthusiastic about what you are selling. *Let your enthusiasm for what you do show!*

It is much easier to convey this kind of enthusiasm when you are speaking to someone face to face, rather than on the phone. For example, your eyes should light up when you talk about your therapy and how much it helps people.

You need to believe in your service in order to sell it - this belief should show on your face. You know what you are selling, because it is what you do; you know everything there is to know about your service. You *do* believe in it, you trained in it, you have spent a lot of time and effort in learning it and you are keen about it. This is good, this is excellent, this is where really effective selling stems from.

The benefits that you offer should be presented in such a way as to be irresistible, so that your client feels attracted and almost compelled by the persuasiveness of your arguments. The customers will then get passionate about what you do, and they are likely to share their enthusiasm with you. This is what you want, because their enthusiasm will interact with yours.

Most of the people who come to shows are quite polite, accepting and open-minded. However, selling face to face will bring up personal issues that you'll need to deal with. You may have anxieties about feelings of rejection and failure, or believe that the public is uncaring, sceptical or even disdainful. You really need to be prepared for this. Even a comment as ineffectual as 'no thanks, I'm not interested' can hurt, because it is a rejection of sorts. You have to learn to deal with this in some way.

You may easily brush off negative comments, or find them quite painful, it depends how deep the feelings of rejection are. You also need to be open to getting feedback from the visitors, the negative along with the positive. Yes, the negative might hurt, but that does not make is any less potentially valid and useful. The other stand holders are good support for this situation. As any person who works with the public knows, sharing your experience with others about people is quite fun, and it's great for dissipating stress.

Don't let this get you down, though. You will meet a lot of interesting people and generally festivals are great fun. You will meet the public, but you'll also meet other stall holders who are probably having to deal with similar issues.

So how do you go about attracting people to your stall? Quite often you will find that people don't come up to your stall, but glance quickly at it as they walk by. You will also notice that most of the people just mill around in certain areas. Visitors to festivals can sometimes be quite shy and may feel awkward about their lack of knowledge about what you do. You need to appear open, receptive and welcoming.

It's good if your stand is very attractive. Spend some time designing your stand before the show, try to make it as professional and slick-looking as possible. The use of colour and props works to attract people to your stall. You may have some sort of demonstration going on at your table, some sort of hands-on activity that people can try out for themselves. Maybe you have some particular tools that you use in your massage that people could try out. You could hold some sort of a contest with a prize for the winners. You could use a banner with an interesting headline:

RELIEVE YOUR PAIN AND HELP OTHERS AT THE SAME TIME

Once you've attracted people to your stall, how do you go about opening a conversation with them? If you are particularly shy, or you don't possess *the gift of the gab*, try to think of some good opening lines. You don't have to be very creative here: 'how are you finding the show?'; 'are there any interesting stands here that I should see'; 'do you know much about aromatherapy?'. These are generally enough to provoke at least a small conversation. Of course, all you have to do is make eye contact with anyone who comes by your table and politely greet them to start some enjoyable chitchat. After all, most of the people are there because they are interested health and want some more information, they just need to be *invited* into your area, so make them feel welcome.

You might consider having a prize draw or a raffle, with a free therapy session as the prize. Get them to fill out a form with their name, address and phone and you could even put them on your mailing list for future use.

One essential accessory to have when you are taking part in a festival is a badge. If the organiser doesn't provide it, design your own. People like to look at badges, and it can help you make your presence felt at the show.

Staff

You probably shouldn't try to run your exhibit on your own. For one thing, being at a show is very demanding and without friendly support it can be stressful. For another, unless you have someone to relieve you, you won't get any breaks. It's a good idea to take a break every couple of hours. It can be an opportunity to wander around the rest of the show and visit other people's stands.

So, you should chose someone you know to be reliable, helpful and friendly to assist you in running your stall. Write up a roster of breaks for you and your staff. Allow time off in the slow periods for wandering around the show, but make sure that someone responsible is left at the stall.

Quite often, the start of a show is really slow. If the show is several days long, the weekdays will be much slower than weekends (unless of course it is a trade show, in which case business hours will be much busier than out of business hours).

Promotional Literature and Flyers

Bring all of the promotional literature that you have. You might also want to print some special leaflets for the festival, perhaps offering a discount to anyone who books a session at the festival. Some people, instead of talking to the folk at the stands, just go around collecting leaflets. The more expensive your leaflets look, the more people will be tempted to pick one up. Refer to the section in this book on *Creating a Great Leaflet* for some ideas on how to plan and design your leaflet for maximum effectiveness.

Be careful if you are taking money from the public. Keep it in a safe place as it's not uncommon for unattended money to disappear very quickly from stalls at festivals. The best idea is to keep the money on your person in the form of a bum bag or money apron. If you decide to have a cash box at your stall, make sure that it is secured to your table and can be locked. It's risky to keep a cash box, so keep an eye on it at all times and warn your staff to look after it too.

Effective Presentation

There's no need to spend a lot of money to make an effective display, what you do need is some creativity and lots of planning ahead time.

First of all, think of an interesting, eye catching, highly visible and easy to read headline or statement. This should go on your stand at eye-level, or somewhere else where it will be noticeable. Ideally, this statement should tell, in a brief and entertaining way, what the main benefits of your therapy are. Make it simple yet effective. Remember that there will be a lot of people who will only glance quickly as they pass by, so keep it short!

If you can, include some visuals at your stand. Diagrams work well, because they can be used as props; you can point to them, walk around them, and explain to the visitors what they are about. This will take away the intensity of continual eye contact. You can get relatively small diagrams blown up to as large as you would like at some specialist photocopying shops. This is quite a cheap service, usually under £20 for a black and white A4 page to go to A0. To enhance this otherwise simple black and white diagram (or poster), you could use paint, coloured pencils, or coloured paper. It is simple but effective, and the results can be quite attractive.

Blown-up photographs, although a bit more expensive, are also a good way of livening up an otherwise boring black and white stall.

Visiting Festivals

If you are not planning to exhibit at a show any time in the near future, why not visit a few? Not as a member of the general public with the intention of buying products or finding out more about services that might be of use to you, but to get some useful tips and ideas for your own business.

You can check out the competition; see what's new on the market; chat with old friends and colleagues and exchange ideas with them; and you can see if it's worthwhile taking a stand in the next show run by those particular organisers. Ask the other stall holders if they've had a good response.

It's worth picking up leaflets from each of the exhibitors. This gives you, in one fell swoop, a range of leaflets with various different designs. It gives you a chance to look at what's on offer in your area and you can look at trends in your field.

The most useful thing about having an up-to-date pile of other people's leaflets, however, is that they can provide you with some ideas for the design, layout and copy of your own brochure.

Before you go to a show, see if you can get hold of a programme. Make a list of the people you want to see. This will save you a lot of time and will also prevent you from wandering around aimlessly.

The best reason to visit exhibitions, however, is to network. See if you can arrange reciprocal referrals with other practitioners whose therapies augment the benefits of your own. At a festival there will be a lot of people who earn their living in a similar way to you, some of them may have some useful ideas on how you can improve your business. Try to meet as many of them as you can, after all, they are all there under one roof and you could make a lot of contacts in a very short period of time.

If you are thinking of setting up your own centre or clinic, a festival is the perfect place to look around for interested and suitable practitioners. Talk to some people about your idea - you could get some very useful feedback.

Don't try to give out your own leaflets to the public while you are there unless you have rented a stall; you will anger the organisers, and this is not a very good networking policy.

Talks and Demonstrations

You can give talks and demonstrations to the public through a variety of channels. Talks are a good way of introducing your therapy to an audience, some of whom may end up being your clients. Your audience are able to view you and hence gain confidence in you. You are able to inform them about what you do, and perhaps give a demonstration if appropriate. Talks are especially good for breaking down barriers, overcoming resistances and allaying fears.

Direct contact with the public will give you useful feedback. It's important to note any fears and apprehensions that people may have about your therapy so that you can address these issues, not only at the talk, but also in your future advertising, leaflets and promotional material.

Setting Up A Talk

You can either set up the talks yourself or get yourself invited to give one. To set up a talk from scratch you will probably need to produce a leaflet to promote it. It may be more cost effective to arrange a series of talks. If you do not have a ready venue, your local library will carry a list of places in your area that can be hired. The library itself may have meeting rooms for hire. You may consider using your own home, or a willing friend may loan you the use of a room. If you are well known in your field then you may already have been invited to give talks.

Try not to make the talk too specialised or involved as this will limit the numbers of people who will be interested in it. Talks which are introductory will catch a bigger audience.

The fee charged to the public should be nominal so that the cost is not a barrier to them showing up. After all, the bigger prize is that they become clients of yours. To this aim you will obviously bring along any leaflets on future workshops and other publicity which you can give to the audience.

Open Days

If you are running a centre then you might consider doing an 'Open Day'. Allocate one day where the public can drop into the centre to sample some of the delights available and to meet some of the practitioners first hand. This is a good method of making yourself known in the local community and can provide you with a forum to practise your networking capabilities! You can make some very useful contacts as well as meeting your potential clients. Consider door-to-door leafleting in your locale to publicise the event as this may work well, as well as some limited advertising. Don't forget to mail your existing clients and invite them to come (and bring a friend).

Adult Education Classes

Running adult education classes can be a way of making money while sowing seeds amongst potential clients in the class (and their acquaintances and friends). The rates of pay are quite reasonable, although not great when you take into account the amount of preparation for the classes that is needed. However, once you have done the preparation for one set of classes, you can use them next time round. Classes tend to be 10 to 30 students in size. The classes are educational, so the teaching aspect as well as demonstrations are important.

Local libraries have lists of adult education classes in your area, or may keep the prospecti on their shelves. If they don't have all the prospecti you can phone the schools to obtain them. From the prospecti you can see where any teaching opportunities may lie. You could then send a CV to the Head of the Adult Education at that school together with a title and outline of the course you would like to teach. You may then be asked for an interview with the Head to discuss the matter further.

Running Workshops

The Concept

Before you plan your first workshop, ask yourself if you are ready to do it. You need a lot of self assurance to be able to plan something six to twelve months in advance and know, absolutely, that you are going to follow through with it. Not only that; if you are not entirely confident about what you are doing, it will show when it comes to facilitating the workshop. Your well-planned, excellently promoted, superbly organised and completely full workshop will not be a success if you are a nervous wreck on the day. Make sure you are ready to embark on this new step in your practice as a therapist.

Naturally, if you are confident that you have something to offer, then there is no reason that, with enough planning and attention to detail, you cannot run a totally successful workshop.

The cardinal rule in running a successful workshop is to *make it your own*. Do what you are best at, address an issue that you think needs addressing, target people who you think you can best help or get through to. However, before you start setting dates, renting out a venue and telling all your peers about it, you should sit down and set down the concept of your workshop on paper.

So what is a concept? Well, once you have defined the purpose of your workshop, the audience that you would most like to have there, and some ideas on what you are going to do then you have your concept. The more complete your concept is, the easier it will be to plan, promote and run the workshop.

For it to be a success, it is imperative that this concept stage take place at least six to nine months before the workshop begins. The main reason that workshops do not fill is because there was not adequate time for promotion and planning. Here are some of the questions that you will want to ask yourself at this point. Keep in mind that it should take more time to read this than to actually commit the answers to paper. If you are seriously considering running a workshop, you may want to get a pen and paper and create your 'concept' now, as you read the following section.

1. Why are you holding this workshop?

Perhaps you need the money. Maybe you need to raise your profile in the area in order to get more individual clients. Maybe running workshops is how you eventually want to 'make your name'. It could be that you have observed some common problems recurring with individual clients and you think that you can best address these problems in the form of a workshop.

There are many reasons to hold workshops, least of all that it focuses your mind, gives you clear goals and deadlines and will bring you some new insights into how you practice your particular form of therapy. You decide why you are doing it; it's your workshop, make it your own.

2. What is it going to be about?

Hopefully, this question will be at least partially answered before you even consider the prospect of holding a workshop. Obviously you are very good at what you do, and you know it. It follows that your workshop will be a showcase of your talents.

So, since you already have some idea of what your workshop is about, commit it to paper. Think of a title. It doesn't have to be the one that you end up using in your promotional material, but it may help to cement the whole theme of the workshop for you.

3. What kind of structure is it going to have?

You now have a *reason* and a title for your workshop. How are you going to present it to the participants? Try to define this briefly and clearly as possible to yourself. You don't have to plan every detail of what you are going to do - that kind of planning will come much closer to the time - but you should have an idea of what form your workshop will take.

You have probably participated in a group setting before, but you may never have held a facilitory role. If this is the case, you need to consider briefly how the group dynamics are going to work. Are you going to run it mainly as a whole group or are you planning on splitting off into smaller groups for part of the workshop? Will you be using any visual techniques such as art therapy or role playing? If you need them, will you be giving demonstrations yourself, will you get someone to come in especially for this purpose, or are you going to ask for volunteers from the group? Commit these elements to paper, because this may help you think of some new and creative ways to run a workshop.

4. Who are you holding it for?

From the outset, you need to clarify *who* you are running your workshop for. There may be many different kinds of people for whom your workshop would be useful, and you need to decide which of these groups of people you want to target. The clearer your idea of the ideal participant is, the easier the promotion and marketing of the workshop will be.

You should also have a general idea of the size you want your workshop to be, taking into account how many people you think you can comfortably handle and how many people you will need to make this venture a financial success.

5. Where, when and how long?

You should have some idea at this point of a venue for the workshop. Ideally you will be familiar with it. If not, you need to make sure that it is big enough, has all of the necessary facilities (enough bathrooms, provision for refreshments, an area for people to get some 'breathing space' if they need it) and is in a reasonably convenient, accessible and attractive location. If your own centre or office would be adequate for the workshop, then you obviously don't have this consideration. How fortunate!

You should also know approximately *when* you want to hold the workshop. Put some thought into this. Therapy, like many 'luxury pastimes', has high seasons and low seasons. If you are unsure of which is which, make a couple of phone calls to other centres and practitioners. You will find out soon enough that the Christmas-New Year season, periods before and after the summer holiday months and bank holidays are not practical times to hold a workshop. In other words, avoid holding workshops during times when it is likely that many people have already made plans.

As far as the length of your workshop, you decide what will work best for you. Maybe a weekend workshop is all your hectic schedule can handle. Maybe you need four days to incorporate all the information and activities you plan into your workshop and find that you can't work two days in a row with the same group. In this case, your workshop could be held every Wednesday evening in November, for example.

Examine the content of the workshop, and your needs as the facilitator, and decide how much time you need and the best times to hold the workshop as far as the participants are concerned.

6. Why?

Why are people going to want to come to your workshop? What are they going to get out of it? Write down the benefits you hope people will receive. Imagine what you'd like to hear people saying to friends about the workshop and how it helped them.

7. Why not?

List all possible reasons that people would *not* come to your workshop and then list all the solutions and arguments you can think of to counter them.

Consider everything, especially when you are thinking of solutions and arguments to get people to come to the workshop. Is your centre in an inconvenient location? Maybe you could rent a bus and provide a shuttle service from a more central place. If you don't consider that to be economically viable, consider how much it would cost you to actually rent a venue for the workshop. Which is the cheaper option, which one the more attractive to potential participants?

Should it happen that you have to hold your workshop at this centre, stress the benefits of participating in a workshop in such a remote place. Is it a peaceful country setting? Can they go for a walk in the nearby national park? Is there a great old fashioned country pub around the corner that serves the best vegetarian shepherd's pie in the county? Instead of ignoring a potential 'problem area' and hoping that nobody notices, turn the liability into an asset.

That is only one example. There are many reasons why people don't come to workshops; they don't like working in groups; there is nothing particularly new or intriguing about your workshop (at least, not in the promotional literature and advertising); it is being held at a particularly bad time; the list goes on and on. For every one of these excuses, you should have a solution, at the ready.

Of all these reasons, though, and all the ones you can come up with on your own, there is only ONE MAJOR reason that people don't attend a workshop: because they haven't heard of it! The only way to counter this is to launch an effective and thorough publicity and advertising campaign.

Budget and Revenue

Before launching straight into how to effectively promote your workshop, a word about money. Obviously money is a serious consideration in all aspects of running a workshop. You want to make a respectable profit and you also need a budget from which to launch your workshop.

The two primary things that your money will be spent on are venue and advertising.

A lot of work goes into locating, booking and preparing a desirable place to hold your workshop. The better the location and the prettier the venue is, the more expensive it will be. If you have to settle for a less than ideal setting, you may want to consider bringing in your own lighting or other cosmetic *quick fixes*. As I have said before, if you already have a suitable venue, then you are one of the lucky ones!

Nevertheless, however difficult and expensive it is to find the right location, it should be twice as difficult and equally expensive to promote and advertise your workshop.

Before you start planning the various ways that you are going to spend your money, give yourself a realistic budget to work with. Obviously you are not going to want to spend £1000 on a workshop that has a projected income of £1000. Neither are you going to want to take out a loan to promote a single weekend workshop. When planning your budget, look at how much money you have available and how much you are expecting to make from the workshop.

Which brings us to the final money topic: what is the projected income from the workshop? Give yourself a wage. If you were doing this for someone else, how much would you be charging? Add to that the projected cost of promoting the workshop (in both time and money) and you should have a fair estimation of what you need to earn. From this you can decide on the size and cost of the workshop. Now it is time to plan the promotion of the workshop.

Promotion and Advertising

In order to fill your workshop, you are going to need to spend a lot of time and energy promoting it. There are two ways of promoting - one that costs money and one that doesn't. Use both. Give yourself deadlines for accomplishing these tasks.

Printing a Leaflet

One of the first things you are going to want to do is get a leaflet or brochure printed. By designing it yourself and writing your own copy you will save a substantial amount of money.

This is where your written concept is going to come in handy. In it you should already have all the elements that you need when creating your leaflet: title, target audience, location and time, the benefits and finally, a list of reasons why people may hesitate to book.

The most crucial elements in your leaflet will be: aiming it at your target audience, stressing the benefits of taking part in the workshop, and allaying any fears or concerns that may prevent people from taking part. If you can convey all of these in a very brief and convincing way, then you have the content (or copy) of your leaflet.

Next comes the design; this includes layout, typesetting, artwork, and type of paper. It may seem that you have endless choice when it comes to designing your leaflet, but many of the choices are made for you when you consider your budget, since a really fancy, glossy, full colour leaflet will probably be far too expensive. If you are as creative as you can be with the resources that you have, the design of your brochure should fall into place.

Getting a printer or freelance designer to design your leaflet for you is quite expensive and you will probably find that there is significantly less money left for fancy paper and colour.

One option is to lay out your brochure on a piece of paper, defining the font (or type style), size of type, margins and paper. You may find a printer that willing to lay out your leaflet to your specifications for little or no extra charge.

Another option is to design your brochure on a computer using a desktop publishing program, assuming you have (or can borrow the use of) a computer and the appropriate software. Most printers will print leaflets from disk. This will cut out the cost of bringing in an outside designer and will allow you to create a leaflet that is much more professional looking than something you might otherwise produce.

Distribution

Getting the leaflet printed is only the first step. No matter how beautiful and fancy it is, it won't do it's job of promoting your workshop unless the right people see it.

You already know who your target audience is, now you need to come up with a list of places that they are likely to gather. If you want to attract working mothers, see if the local nurseries, will display a pile of your brochures in their foyers. Looking to recruit people for your workshop 'Improve your Vision the Natural Way'? Why not try distributing your leaflets to local optometrists?

You should distribute your leaflets to as many places as you can find where it will be taken for free. Many health food stores, libraries, theatres and cafes have either notice boards or shelves for displaying leaflets (although it is advisable to get someone's permission before you drop off a pile of expensive brochures, since they could end up in the bin at the end of the day).

Another way of getting your leaflet distributed is through distribution agencies, although this is a more expensive option, to be considered only by those holding more expensive workshops.

If you have a mailing list, you should consider doing a mail out of the leaflet. You can also buy mailing lists. See the section on *Leaflets* for further information on distribution.

Advertising

Once you have decided when you are going to hold your workshop, you should immediately look into buying advertising. It's vital that you get the timing right, especially if you plan on advertising in quarterly or monthly publications.

Make a list of the papers that you would like to advertise in and commit yourself to an advertising budget. If you have printed up your leaflet, you may find that you do not have that much money left over for buying advertisements. Perhaps you can only afford to buy small box adverts in two publications. If this is the case, decide whether it is worth it.

If you have held a workshop before, you should know exactly the kind of response you got from previous advertising you have bought. If you have never advertised before, ask other practitioners what kind of response they have had from advertising in a particular newspaper or magazine.Refer to the section on *Creating a Great Advert* for more ideas.

Free Self Promotion

This is the cheapest and most rewarding method of promoting yourself, but also the most time consuming.

There are an unlimited number of methods of free self promotion. Here are some ideas:

• **Get your workshop included in listings magazines.**

You will have to find out what listings magazines cover your area, how often each one is printed and the copy deadline for the issues.

• **Get yourself in the paper.**

To do this, you will have to send out a press release. Refer to the section on *Press Releases* for information on how to produce one that will get responses.

• **Get yourself interviewed on television on or the radio.**

This works along the same lines as getting your name in print, but you will have to make your workshop seem interesting, newsworthy and relevant.

• **Become known by other practitioners and health centres in the area**

Do some legwork. Go and introduce yourself to all the doctors, health clinics, natural health practitioners and fitness centres in the area. See if you can leave them some leaflets, maybe in exchange for displaying their leaflets or brochures at your practice. This method of self-promotion may not result in immediate bookings, but it will give you increased name recognition for future promotion.

• **Get other practitioners to refer their patients to your workshop.**

While you are doing your legwork, why not ask the GPs and other natural health practitioners to refer certain clients to your workshop. You may find that they are quite open to the idea if your therapy is complementary to theirs. If they want to see a workshop for themselves before they refer their clients, invite them along. The more well known you become, even if it is only locally, the easier future self promotion will be.

• **Send out tapes of former workshops.**

Technically, This is not FREE self promotion, but it is quite low cost to record your workshop and then pick out some appropriate sessions to use as samples. You may even want to send these samples to people who have responded to your ads and leaflets.

Obviously if you are considering recording a workshop to use as future promotional material, you will need permission from all of the participants. You might want to get this permission by getting your clients to sign a consent form. This probably won't work for psychotherapy, but would be a good idea for other, less sensitive therapies. If you use music, or voice therapy, or want to record yourself verbally leading the group in visualisation or relaxation then a tape would be an appropriate promotional medium.

- **Get yourself involved in a controversial activity**

This is only for the hardened renegade self-promoter, but if you are using a controversial technique in your therapy, or you happen to be extra curricularly involved in some other form of controversial activity, use this to get your name in the paper. After all, any publicity is good publicity. Of course, this is a very risky venture, and might work against you.

The Workshop

As far as running a successful workshop goes, you should be quite confident that you can do this. Be as professional as possible. This means you must be punctual, arriving before any of the participants arrive and staying until after it has finished in case anyone has questions or concerns.

Have a schedule written up, especially if you are incorporating many different activities into one day's work. Stick to this schedule as strictly as is possible, but don't be a slave to it, as this can inhibit your creativity and spontaneity. Some workshop leaders work best when they have the first third to half well timed and prepared, and then let the 'process' take over. You have to find which mix of structure and openness works best for you as a workshop leader. This kind of openness, however, does not mean that you are unprepared. It requires considerable skill to work with the group process.

Make sure that you have included enough break-time in the schedule. Take a breather at least every two hours and you will avoid any significant drops in concentration levels.

Be organised. Know exactly what you are going to say and do. This is especially useful if you are nervous about holding the workshop. Obviously you cannot know in advance exactly how people are going to react, or how well they are going to participate. However, if you know your *script* well enough, you'll have the confidence you need to deal with small deviations from your plans.

Be prepared for anything. If you feel the need, practice parts of the workshop with your partner, your children or your friends. Imagine some 'worst case client' scenarios and then imagine some solutions.

Evaluating your Workshop

You should evaluate your workshop both with the participants and later, on your own. There are many ways of getting feedback about the workshop with the participants. You may want to get them to fill in a form. Maybe you or one of the participants could lead an evaluating 'brainstorm', either writing the ideas down on paper or recording them. You could hold an optional post-workshop evaluation with a structured evaluation setting to start off with and a looser party-like atmosphere after that. You may simply want to host a follow-up party a couple weeks after the workshop and get some feedback in a very informal way.

However you do it, you really should get some feedback from the clients. Find out what their expectations were on coming to the workshop. What did they like and dislike about the workshop, the structure, the timing, the *group dynamic*? Were their expectations met, or did they come away with something totally different, but just as valuable? Do they think that what they learned in the workshop is going to affect their everyday lives? The more information you get from them, the more you can improve your next workshop.

You also need to evaluate the workshop for yourself. Did you fill the workshop? If yes, how do you think you did this. If not, what did you fail to do. What kind of people came to the workshop? Did the participants consist mostly of your 'target group'? Were you surprised at what kind of people came to your workshop? What promotional method attracted the most participants? Which ads got the most response? Which ones, if any, got no response?

It's vital that you sit down and answer all of these questions. The success of your next workshop, and the evolution of your own practice, depend on it. Good luck!

Notice Boards

Many therapists begin by advertising on notice boards in their local area. This is a cheap, simple way of promoting yourself. The effectiveness of sticking your card, leaflet or poster on a notice board depends on the where you put it, what it looks like and what it says.

The best notice boards are going to be in places that your potential clients visit. Although corner shops are used by a large number of people, only a small percentage of the customers will be interested in your alternative therapy. Notice boards in health food shops and natural health centres will be read by a greater number of people who are likely to be interested in what you do. So take some time to consider where your potential clients are likely to go and then put your ads up where they will see them. Health centres, health food shops and cafes, local libraries and sports centres often have notice boards for community services, local activities and practices.

Be careful if you are a body therapist, particularly if you work from home. Many people advertising massage, for example, mean something completely different. It could be distressing to deal with calls from people who have misinterpreted your ad. Carefully choosing where to display your ads will help in avoiding this situation as will your choice of words. Emphasise your professional qualifications. Female practitioners may choose to advertise 'women only' and to work only with men who are referred to you.

What you say will be dictated by the size of your ad. Many notice boards display business cards which state the basic information. Your name, address of where you practise, phone number, your therapy and qualifications are essential information and will fit on a business card. You can get business cards printed very cheaply on machines in train stations and post offices. That's fine but on a notice board covered in business cards you need something to make your card stand out. Using colours and logos can make *your card* more eye-catching and so more effective.

Fliers and leaflets are a better way of advertising on notice boards as you can give more information about yourself and your practice and so have more opportunity to interest and attract clients. More space means bigger and bolder and so more eye-catching.

The cost of advertising on a notice board is relatively low and depends largely on the cost of making your ad. It is worth spending money to make your ad stand out and be noticed. It is free to advertise on many notice boards. Charges are minimal.

Only advertise on local boards. You are less likely to attract people who have to travel far to get to you and it will cost you too much in time and money to display ads far from your practice. Don't expect an enormous response. As with all forms of advertising a 1% response rate is a success.

Notice boards are a cheap way of getting your name and practice noticed in your local vicinity and can be a valuable part of your advertising strategy especially if you are having cards or leaflets printed anyway.

Even More Creative Marketing

Get Testimonials of Celebrities

One interesting way to promote yourself is to offer your services to celebrities, people that are well-known in your field or people that are widely known to the public (if you have the opportunity). If you are confident in your abilities as a therapist, you could offer them a session, or offer to let them take part in a course for free. It's a bit of a gamble, but if they like it then they will be able to testify to the effectiveness of your therapy. There's nothing for promoting yourself like being able to say 'Recommended by Princess Diana'.

This is an especially useful method if you are in the business of training other therapists. It would be a relatively easy thing to engage someone who is well-known in your field, but perhaps not necessarily a nationwide celebrity. When you have a testimonial from a reputable practitioner in your field (you could even go as far as calling this person a *colleague*), someone that potential students would probably have heard of, then they will feel confident about choosing to train with you.

Barter

It might be profitable to consider visiting your local new age shop, aromatherapy shop, vegetarian cafe, independent cinema or any place where quite a lot of people congregate. Offer to do some promotional swaps with them. You could get a cafe to print an A4 sized poster for your upcoming weekend workshop on the back of their menu in exchange for a place on your workshop. You could get a printer to print up some lovely promotional material in exchange for three months' worth of free massage therapy. Bartering is older than money, and its uses are endless. Take advantage of it.

Setting up a Training Programme

Setting up a training programme is a very big step which you may be considering for a number of reasons. Perhaps teaching is your long-term goal. It could be that you have been a therapist for a number of years and are finding that you prefer to work in groups rather than with individual clients. Perhaps you are a well-established practitioner who feels a need to move on to a greater challenge. Or perhaps you just feel that you need to diversify your work for financial and creative reasons.

Where to start

If you are thinking of establishing your own training centre, there are a number of serious considerations to be made. What kind of premises are you going to need to run it? How much capital do you have to invest in this new business? Are you going to do this on your own or with partners? In what capacity do you want to be involved with the training centre, as trainer or as co-ordinator?

If you want to set up training for a body therapy such as yoga, acupuncture or massage there are other considerations. What sort of equipment will you need? Are you going to need specially qualified staff (first aid training, etc.)? Then there are the other details such as how students are going to pay and what supplies they are going to need.

Why Bother?

Of course, for the first five years of running a newly established training practice, you will experience some birthing pains, but there are many long-term rewards to running your own programme. Not least of all is that you will become more well known, gaining much prestige and authority as more of your students establish themselves as therapists in their own right.

You will also find that as the years go by you will meet (and train) many more therapists, both in your particular field of therapy and in other disciplines. This will not only help to bolster your reputation, but hopefully it will also provide you with a support network, a group of people you can turn to when you are feeling burnt-out, or when you need some feedback from an outside source. Of course, this network will also turn to you, and knowing other therapists will provide you with an opportunity to engage in supervisory work. Ideally you will also give each other referrals from time to time.

Having your own centre will also give you much greater financial security. As well as training fees, you will have other sources of income such as supervision fees, individual client fees, income from workshops and whatever other sidelines you choose.

Since you will be marketing to a very specific group of people - that is, people who want to, and can afford to, change their careers and train in your particular type of therapy - you will find that your marketing is much easier. You are also one of a relatively small group of businesses, or the only business, that offers the kind of training *you* do. This will enable you use the 'The Positive Way' (see the section on *Setting Your Fees*).

What Birthing Pains?

Finding good premises in a suitable location is a major consideration. You are going to need somewhere that is big enough for training, you will also need office/administration space, enough bathroom facilities and probably a kitchen or kitchenette. In short, you are looking for a building the size of a small house, but one that has at least the potential to become a professional space. Remember the golden rule: *Locate your premises where potential clients live or work.*

You could run the centre out of your own home if it is big enough, but it will have to be in a relatively central location. Alternatively, you may want to move, buying another home that will happily accommodate both your private and professional lives. Again, you will want a space that feels like a 'centre' and not like the downstairs half of a crowded house. Many trainings run from rented premises too, where groups are held in rented rooms and the administration is done from someone's home. You could even look into buying an existing practice and premises. If you can find a promising practice with an established clientele, there will be considerably less set up costs.

Setting up your own centre, then, is going to require quite a lot of capital, and not just to secure premises. You are going to have a lot of administration work to do, if not immediately after establishing your centre, then at least some time in the not so distant future. For this you will need equipment: a business phone, a computer and relatively high quality printer, and probably a fax machine (which may require another phone line). If you are thinking of running most of the courses yourself, you will also need an administration staff. It's not a good idea to try to run the whole show on your own. If you do, you will probably find that in a matter of months most of the administration work has become disorganised, and you are behind in responding to enquiries, invoicing your students, buying the necessary supplies, paying your bills and keeping your accounts accurate and up to date.

If you are short of capital and administration staff, one solution is to set up the training centre with two or three (the more the merrier) other interested parties. Approach people who you know you can work with, who share your basic philosophy, and people who have good reputations and, ideally, recognised qualifications, academic or otherwise. If you cannot find enough interested parties who practice your particular form of therapy, consider establishing a multi-discipline centre.

If you cannot find any suitable partners, and you are determined to set up a training practice with limited capital, then you will have to start off small, perhaps seeing individual clients for your main source of income and running a single one-year course for a couple of years. Build up your reputation and your skills at training before you try to find larger, more glamorous facilities. After a couple of years of running a small training centre on your own, you may find it quite easy to get other parties interested in investing.

One thing you *will* find about running your own centre is how much work is involved. On top of running your courses and seeing individual clients, there will be a lot of work to be done with regards to planning your curriculum, evaluating students, following up on past students, etc. This will have to be reflected in your fees. Good luck!

Creating a Sideline

One way to branch out as a practitioner is to create a sideline. The most obvious sidelines are books, videos and audio cassettes, but there are others, such as selling essential oils or incense. Although such a venture may seem daunting prospect, when looked at more closely it is not very difficult to do and carries enormous benefits.

What are the benefits?

Publicity

Having your own book, video or tape is a great form of publicity. You will be able to reach many more potential clients by branching out in this way. Your name will become recognised more widely. This opens up the market enormously. Some people may prefer to discover more about your therapy in the privacy of their own home and through books, tapes and videos.

Becoming a figure of authority

Having written a book about a subject immediately puts you in a different position as a practitioner; people will see you as an authority on the subject; people may well turn to you for information and will value your opinion; you will be in a better position to offer training courses and workshops. These new opportunities may lend themselves to even more sideline work. So it goes on: your client list grows, students abound and you sell your sideline to more and more people.

Better income

Creating a sideline brings in extra money. If you are lucky, your book may become a best-seller. In turn, the more recognised your name becomes, the more clients you will attract.

There are many different ways to sell a product. Your publisher/distributor should be selling your product, but that shouldn't stop you from selling by mail order catalogue and appropriate retail outlets such as bookshops and health food shops. At festivals, you could sell your new sideline products on a rented stand, distribute your leaflets, meet and talk to prospective clients and offer demonstrations and taster treatments. The festival may present an opportunity to promote yourself through talks, workshops or demonstrations to the public.

Which sideline for you.

What sort of sideline you create depends largely on what you do. Some practices can be more effectively presented on video, for example, than others. Audio cassettes lend themselves to the promotion of self-help techniques like hypnotherapy, meditation, vocal work and visualisation. Tapes to help people stop smoking, overcome insomnia and beat stress using these techniques are popular and effective.

There are many other products you could market. Think of what it is that your clients might be interested in buying. If you are an aromatherapist or masseur you could sell your own essential oils. If you are a crystal healer you could sell a range of crystals. Herbalists could successfully produce and sell their own remedies. If you can get the raw products at a discount this could be a very profitable venture. Your clients will be happy to buy the remedies from you rather than have to make another journey to get them elsewhere. Nutritionists and dieticians can buy vitamin, mineral and other food supplements at wholesale price from a number of big brand names if you register as a therapist with them. Selling these products are not only a form of publicity for yourself, but enables you to offer your clients a better service.

Publishing and promoting your book

Writing a book takes time, time to research and time to write. You will need a word processor to do this. Once you have completed the final draft, the next task is to find a publisher or to publish your book yourself. Several hundred new age/ holistic health titles are published each year in the UK so as you can imagine competition is fierce and finding an interested publisher takes perseverance and patience. In the UK, approximately 50,000 new titles are published each year.

Cassells Directory of Publishing lists most of the publishers in the UK. You will probably find a copy in your local library. Look in the health section of your local bookshops, the name of the publisher will be on the book covers, it shouldn't be too difficult to find a few publishers who specialise in your type of book.

Avoid 'vanity publishers' who expect authors to completely finance the publishing of their books. With these publishers, you are asked to pay thousands of pounds in advance to cover publishing and printing costs, and they usually make enormous profits from your gullibility. They don't have a good reputation in the trade because their books are often of poor quality, they do little to promote their books and are primarily money-making schemes.

There is an effective strategy for approaching publishers, but do be prepared for refusals and don't take them personally. Be confident in your work and determined and you will get there in the end. Your chances of finding a publisher who is prepared to take the financial risk of publishing your work will be greater if you follow these rules.

Write a synopsis of your work

A synopsis of your book should includes the following; a short description of your target audience and why your book would appeal to them; the title of your book; your name, address and telephone number. This will be invaluable when approaching potential publishers.

Alternatively, instead of a synopsis you could send a summary of each chapter and an outline.

Ask others to read your manuscript

It is hard to be objective about your own work. The more people who read your manuscript the better. Listen to people's comments and allow them to help you to improve your work. Try to get the opinions of people who are renowned in your field. You can briefly quote their remarks in your synopsis to support your book.

Make sure your manuscript is clearly presented

It should be clearly typed, double spaced with wide margins and on one side of the paper only.

Research possible publishers

Draw up a list of possible publishers. Find out what other books they publish and how many new titles they publish annually. Bookshops that stock their books will be able to help you with this and will be able to give you an idea of how well the books sell.

It's a good idea to make personal contact with the publisher if possible.

A brief phone call before you send in your manuscript makes all the difference. Call each prospective publisher and talk to whomever deals with new authors. Describe your work and target audience. If they are interested, ask that person how they would like your work to be submitted. Some publishers want the whole manuscript, some want the synopsis, and others prefer the first chapter and a table of contents.

When you are requested to send something in to a publishing house, do it immediately. Address it to the person you have spoken with and mention your recent conversation. Give them three weeks and then phone again to make sure they've received your work. They may not have had a chance to read it, so offer to call again and make a date. If they have read it, ask for their opinions and ideas. Discuss how you could change things to accommodate them. If they don't consider your book suitable for them, ask if they could recommend another publisher who, they think, would be interested.

Normally, you will receive publisher's decisions by letter. Don't be put off by rejection. Many good manuscripts are rejected because publishers are already fully committed or because your book is not the sort of thing they normally publish. They may not address the market that your book is intended for. Stay positive and approach the next publisher on your list. Start the conversation by thanking them for reading your manuscript. Be careful to remain calm as you don't want to earn yourself the reputation of being 'a difficult author to be avoided'.

When your manuscript is accepted, you will be offered a contract with your publisher. If this is your first book, you can expect to receive approximately a thousand pounds in advance royalties (the actual sum is dependent on many factors). On the sale of each book, you will receive about ten percent of the cover price on hard back books and eight percent for paperbacks. About 30-35% goes to the bookshop, 15-25% goes to the distributor, the publishers get the remainder. It is the publishing company that has to pay for printing (about fifteen percent), production and promotion costs including staff, all the overheads associated with running a business (about twenty percent), and your royalties (about ten percent). When this is added up, the publishers - the ones who take all the financial risks - actually only make about five percent profit.

When you sign a contract with a publisher, you agree to let them take responsibility for the production process. Your work may be heavily edited and you may be asked to make changes. The cover design may be far from what you would have chosen personally. Don't get upset, remember that the publisher's main focus is to produce a commercially successful book.

There are things you can do to help promote the book. Communicate with your publisher about this. The more co-operative and enthusiastic you are the better. This will rub off on your publisher and encourage them to promote your book more energetically.

Publishing yourself

Since desktop publishing has become affordable and simple systems are widely available, publishing your own book is a possibility. Remember that the production and printing of the book is only part of the job. You may need to pour a lot of time and energy into promoting your book to get it selling.

Use a Computer

Have your edited final version on computer disc and check it for spelling and grammatical errors. You can use any word processor compatible with the desktop publishing (DTP) system you intend to use. If your word processor or floppy disk format is not compatible with the DTP system you want to use you can get your disk converted to a compatible format for up to £20.

Desktop Publishing

You can either use DTP yourself or give it to someone else to do. Remember to use a universal page size to keep your printing costs down. If you're not sure of what size to use just measure a typically sized book and copy that. Use an easy to read font such as 'Palatino', size nine point. This can be printed by most Postscript laser printers, from which you can produce camera-ready art work. You can get ideas on design and layout from other books

Cover Design

Books are primarily judged by their covers, especially if the author is not well known. Bear this in mind when you design your cover. Use full colour to make your design more eye catching. Both bookshops and their customers are attracted to books by their covers. When deciding which books to have in stock a bookshop, the buyer will take only five seconds, on average, to decide. Predictably then, this decision is based entirely on the appearance of the book. Reps only carry covers with them so it's not as if the buyer even has a chance to flick through the book to see what it's about. Customers in book shops usually buy on impulse. The title must grab their interest so that even the spine of the book has the power to attract attention. Use large letters that contrast with the colour of the spine, a catchy title and your name, especially if you are well known in your field.

A good subtitle will also help attract readers' attention. The back page is your prime selling space. Here you can really catch your readers' interest and make them want to find out more. You can also use this as an opportunity to inspire confidence with some reassuring testimonials.

It's money well spent if you get a professional graphic designer with some experience in books to design your cover for you. Find some book covers that you like and ask the designer to produce something as striking. Get several hundred extra covers printed which can be given to sales reps or used for publicity purposes.

Printing

You will need to know how many pages your book is going to have before getting a quote from a printer. Include title pages, contents, index, dedication and a few spare blank pages at the end too. Books are usually printed onto a large sheet of paper with sixteen or thirty two pages to a sheet, which is then cut and folded into the finished size. Adjust the number of pages to fit multiples of sixteen or thirty two by changing your page layout.

Try several commercial printers for quotes. They will need to know the number of pages and page size. Most printers offer recycled paper which is more expensive than paper made from virgin wood. There is an argument that the chemicals used in recycling are more damaging to the environment than producing new paper. So if you agree with this idea then you could make donations to tree planting schemes to ease your conscience.

Marketing and promotion

Approach magazines, radio, newspapers and magazines for book reviews. The more the merrier.

Pricing and trade terms.

If you sell to bookshops directly the norm is to give them a thirty to thirty five percent discount off the cover price. For single copies you can offer a twenty five percent discount. Usually you pay for delivery. You can also offer a 'sale or return' deal to encourage shops to carry more stock.

If you sell through a distributor, you will have to give them about fifteen percent of the cover price as well as the booksellers' discount. Invoice immediately, specifying standard terms of payment of thirty days. If you don't receive your money in this time, send a polite reminder letter.

Making and Marketing a Video

Video is a great medium for promoting your practice. Many people prefer to relax in front of a screen and be fed information through images and narrative. Certain practices like traditional Thai massage, for example, can be difficult to explain in writing and through diagrams, but the techniques can be simply and clearly illustrated on film. Such videos can be used as a valuable resource in training courses and workshops and also as a visual aid for lectures, demonstrations, conferences and exhibitions.

When choosing a video production company you need to spend some time looking around for the right one. Ask to see their show reels to get an idea of the kind of work they've done before, and to see the quality of their production. Ask the producers as many questions as you can think of, in particular about the budget and whether it was on target, the schedule and whether it was produced on time. You can also ask previous clients if they were happy with their programme and the production company.

Many people are put off the idea of making a video when a production company quotes a huge cost. There are ways of reducing the costs of production such as using cheaper video formats. So don't despair, ask about the possibilities of using a cheaper format.

To ensure a video is produced efficiently and with minimum expense, it is essential that the script is well researched and well written. Pre-production meetings are the place and time to express your ideas on what the video is about and who the target audience are. Make sure there is a good understanding and clear communication between you and the production company to avoid their dictating the content of your video. It is better to start out with this understanding than to try to rectify things at the editing stage. At least the director and script writer should share your ideas and be sympathetic to your business or product. Working with like-minded people will make life a lot easier.

Although making a video yourself may be an attractive low-cost idea, is not a good idea unless you have the skills and experience to produce a good quality programme. Anything less is likely to put potential customers off rather than attract them to your practice.

Not all practices can be easily presented in a visual way. If this is the case, then you'll need a good story or analogy to get your message across. Make sure the video is interesting and entertaining. Watch other practitioners videos at exhibitions and any other opportunities, to get an idea of what works and what doesn't.

Producing and selling audio cassettes and CDs.

There are two main issues involved in producing a successful tape or CD; is it what they want? And are they going to buy it?

What do people want?

First of all you must define your project. Write exactly what you want to convey in a short concise statement. Once you have defined your project you can make sure every part of the process is leading towards that goal. Think about who your audience is and research this market. Now that you have defined your project and the market make sure your assumptions are correct by asking people within this group if they would be interested in your tape or CD. Find out how much they would be prepared to pay for it, and where they would go to buy it. Be open to criticism and listen to people's ideas.

When it comes to distributing your tape or CDs there are a number of options to consider. You can approach high street shops. You can also make your book available through mail-order catalogues, by advertising in specialist magazines and at specialist outlets like health food shops and festivals.

The production process

Recordings can be done at home or in a recording studio. You will find a list of recording studios in the yellow pages. If your project involves speech, make sure your script is perfect before you go into the studio. Time in the studio costs money. You may want to use your own voice on the recording. Consider whether your voice is suitable for the subject you are discussing. If not, it's worth getting someone else to do it. Even if most of the tape's content is to be verbal, music is valuable in making the recording more interesting. Sometimes just listening to a voice can become very monotonous. You can use music from a music library which good studios will have access to. The cost of this music depends on what you are using it for and how much you use.

If you are only recording speech then there is no need to rent expensive multi-track studios you can hire a cheaper facility, a 4- or 8-track studio. If you are recording from a live performance it is important that the original recording is of a high a quality as possible so that the copies are also of good quality. Invest in producing a high quality master tape. The master tape should be reel to reel 1/4 inch tape or a digital format like DAT. The maximum time available for each side of a tape is 50 minutes so be careful not to exceed this unless you intend to produce more than one tape.

Producing compact discs involves highly specialised production facilities which make them comparatively expensive. Also few CD manufacturers will consider orders of less than 100 units.

When packaging your finished product you have to compete with an enormous market. Your cover design must be eye catching if it is to attract buyers. Look at other designs and get an idea of what works and what doesn't. Take some ideas to a graphic designer to produce a professional looking cover.

Promotion

You need to draw people's attention to your product to boost sales. The media have sections specially for reviewing products or works that they think will be of interest to their readers. To promote your product, get editorial in these reviews. Send review copies of your tape to anyone who might be interested. Send a press release at the same time explaining who you are, what your product is and any other relevant information. Approach local and national press, magazines, specialist productions, radio and television.

Advertise in places that interested prospective buyers are going to look such as specialist publications. It is easy to waste money on advertising. Design your advertising carefully and don't use too many words. Keep it clear and simple. It is better to test the water first with smaller ads.

How To Sell Yourself

You probably hate the thought of selling. More likely than not, this is because when you think of selling, you think of people who won't take 'no' for an answer. People like the Jehovah's Witnesses who, even when you make it blatantly clear that you are not interested, will stand on the doorstep for eternity. Of course you resent this. You may even end up slamming the door in their face.

Often the image that springs to mind is of a hard, pushy salesperson often trying to talk someone into buying something they don't want. This approach to promotion is actually very ineffective, especially in the therapeutic field, because it rarely ends in a sale!

Don't Sell, Just Let Them Buy

What do I mean by this? Well, you buy things every day, we all do. You go down to your local shop or pop into the local supermarket and buy some groceries. By definition, the supermarket is selling to you, but it doesn't feel like they're selling to you, they're just making it *easier* for you to buy. Shops have a lot of ways of making it easier for you to buy.

Not long ago there were no such thing as self-service shops. You had to place your order over the counter, item by item, with a queue forming behind you. Not very convenient and not exactly conducive to spending loads of money. Buying became a lot easier when self service stores were introduced; the variety and selection of goods multiplied astronomically, while packaging, placement and pricing of the goods became the selling points. Selling products has become an art, not the art of forcing people to buy things, rather the art of making buying very easy.

50% of the people who ring you up about your therapy are already 'sold'. The others simply want to find out a bit more information to satisfy their curiosity. The selling that is involved in this field, then, only accounts for about 50% of enquiries.

Why is this? It's because, just like the supermarket, you've made it easy for them to buy! You've done the work on the promotional material that they are responding to. You are there when they phone you. Perhaps you have a reputation that precedes you. You've arranged your timetable to make it easy to book people in. In a sense you've laid the foundations that make it easy for them to buy. All they are doing now is ringing up to make a booking, or they've got some queries that need answering.

Here is a list of general rules which come in handy when you are trying to clinch the final half, the 50% who still need convincing that your therapy is the one they need.

Rule #1: Wait to be invited

Don't sell. Don't push. Don't come out with some spiel about how good your therapy is and why it's so great for them...until you know what they want. It's important that you wait for them to invite you to talk about your therapy. They may ask a question like "I've got a problem with my lower back, is the Alexander Technique effective in treating this kind of problem?" There is your invitation to offer some information about your practice, and a chance to say honestly how you think your particular method of working can be of use to them.

You do need to find out, when they phone up, what it is they really want. To do this, you might want to ask them some questions first; remember, it is much more useful to know your client's needs before you start telling them what you offer, otherwise you may find that you have wasted your time trying to sell them something that they may not actually want.

A word of warning: the quickest way to lose someone's interest is to start selling them something before you know what they want. The trick is to find out what it is that your potential client really wants.

Rule #2: Listen to What Your Clients Are Saying

Although each client is an individual, there is some central reason they have for coming to see you that they probably share with thousands of other people. It is worth listening to what your clients tell you because they are your market, they hold all of the information about who your market is, who to target when it is time to get more clients.

Every therapist gets complaints from clients. Don't be afraid to listen to these gripes. Often these clients have a different perspective on what you do and have good, solid ideas about how you can improve your service. If a lot of your clients are complaining that your practice is too far to travel to, look at where they live. Maybe many of your clients live quite a short distance from each other but quite far from your practice. You could consider moving your practice, or renting a room in that area on certain days of the week. If a large proportion of your clients live in a certain area, this tells you that it would be a good location to set up a practice, or, if that's not a feasible option, you could consider stepping up promotion in that area. Perhaps the fact that many of your clients come from far away is an indication that you should try concentrating your promotion closer to home.

If many of clients say they would like to bring their partner in to the therapy sessions, consider training in couple counselling and offering this as a service.

If your clients are telling you that they could do with a neck and shoulder massage at work, you could offer to meet them at work every Thursday afternoon for a slightly higher fee. You could enquire at their company, as to whether there are other people who would be interested in getting a massage during working hours! That would add a whole new dimension to your business.

Rule #3. Explain How You Can Help

Once you've found out what the particular needs of your potential clients are, then you need to match the service you offer to suit those needs. You must tell them how your therapy can help their particular problem. You will highlight the benefits of your therapy, knowing that they will satisfy the particular concerns of your potential client.

You must address their particular problems, and their concerns, but this can be done in a positive way. For instance:

• if the client suffers from headaches, and they want to know if your herbal treatment helps alleviate headache pain, don't explain how wonderfully cheap your herbal treatment is in comparison to other form of therapy. Instead give them an example of someone you have helped with headache pain, or any other deep physical pain for that matter;

• if their main concern is being helped in relating with other people better, don't tell them how your counselling practice is renowned for promoting 'self-discovery', but rather how this self-discovery will bring about a revolution in the way that they interact with other people;

• if the client's concern is that your practice is too far away for them to get to, don't focus on how wonderfully effective your therapy is, tell them of other clients who live even farther away and have been continually coming to you for some time because your therapy is so effective. Invite them to make the journey for one session and see for themselves how accessible it is by car or public transport;

• if the client is worried that they will be in therapy for a seemingly interminable length of time, don't focus on how therapy will make them feel so much better, instead emphasise the fact that the length of time that any one client stays in therapy depends upon a number of factors, including a level of co-operation between therapist and client and the desire of the client to effect changes in their life.

If the customer has more than one concern, address the most important one first. When a potential client does express concerns you may want to ask them why that particular concern is so important to them. This will help you to find out more about what their specific needs are.

Some people like to have a script handy by the phone. You have to be very careful with this tactic because although the idea of the script might be to cover the important points, it can never respond to the individual needs and queries of each customer. I would suggest that if you are going to use a script, use it wisely and sparingly. You don't really want to fall into the lazy habit of giving the same description of your activities to every caller. You will need to have a number of different ways to explain your service, each explanation tied to each individual customer.

Handling Objections to Your Fees

When potential clients express a concern about cost, often their objection isn't about cost at all but more to do with the appropriateness or effectiveness of your therapy. The client doesn't really think that therapy is going to benefit them. So objections about price are actually objections about value. Once you understand this, it's a question of finding the particular need of that client and explaining how your therapy will benefit them.

In response to this you have a number of options. You could say "Well, yes, I'm the most expensive therapist in town" and if they ask why, you can respond, "I'm the best and many people are willing to pay high prices in exchange for such effective therapy". Essentially what you have to sell is value. Maybe your therapy is worth more because you have been practising for longer or you have more training than most therapists, maybe you are trained in several different kinds of therapy. If you can explain this, and match this information with any other concerns this particular client has, then you will be dealing with their main concerns and gradually taking away their reasons for not coming to an introductory session.

Practitioners often feel uneasy about charging for their services, but charging money sets a boundary - it reminds clients that you are not their friend, and that you are conducting a business transaction. Many clients who have their fees paid by insurance companies, mysteriously get better as soon as the insurance money runs out and they have to pay for it themselves. I've heard many statements from therapists doubtful about the whole process of charging. There include:

'I don't take money personally from clients, I get the receptionist to take the money for me'.

'Everybody should get treatments for free'.

'The more I charge, the more pressure I feel to produce the *goods* and I hate to work under such pressure'.

'Is what I do good enough to charge so much?'

'I can't possibly charge more than my therapist (or supervisor) charges'.

'I can't bear my clients reactions to putting up price'.

'My circle of friends would frown on me if I charged more than I presently do'.

'Nobody will come if I charge above the going rate'.

'Charging money fixes me to a treatment schedule and I hate working to a fixed time limit'.

Some positive comments I've heard are:

'I deserve it'.

'When I'm paid it makes me feel like what I do is of value'.

'I like to see the cash put on the palm of my hand'.

'I feel great when all this money comes in'.

'It gives me a thrill to earn my living doing therapy'.

'I've done a long training and I deserve every penny I get'.

Like sex, money is full of emotion and contradiction. Asking someone how much money they make in a year is about as tactful as asking them how often they masturbate. Not surprisingly it's hard to set fees and to respond to other people's reactions to your fees without some sense of unease.

It's important that you feel comfortable about your fees and confident that your services are worth what you are charging. If you consistently charge less than your peers, it may be worth considering working on your own level of self esteem.

If you are recently qualified and are just starting to practise, the jump from practising on friends or charging very low fees to charging full fees can be a big one. Essentially, it's a move from being an amateur to becoming a professional, that's a big mental leap forward! You must charge a realistic fee for your service, after all, you are now trying to make a living from practising your therapy.

Cannot Afford Your Fees

Sometimes, however, a client will have a genuine money problem and can't actually afford your service. If this is the case, and they are on benefits, a student or an OAP for instance, ask them how much they can afford. If you are not willing to offer them a concession, then there is really nothing you can do for this person. However, if you are going to offer a concession, don't offer it straight away.

Think about what can be given in return for this concession. Maybe they can come in at odd hours, or you can have a stand-by system, whereby the client can fill in for *no shows*. There may be a particular time of day that is usually very slow for you and they could fill this for you. Perhaps you could use the bartering system, get them to build some shelves or paint your office in exchange for a few sessions. Sometimes people have savings, or a parent who is willing to pay for treatment. If they are low-waged, can they get extra work to pay for treatment? You could take on the client with the agreement that when they find work, or their income goes up past a certain level, then they must start paying full price.

It's up to you to work this out, and it's vital that you discuss all of the details of payment honestly and clearly before you start seeing the client. Make sure before you agree on anything that you are both comfortable with the agreement. It's irritating to give concession to someone on the dole, only to find them wanting the next three sessions off so they can fly to Barbados for a holiday.

However, before you are surprised by any requests for concessions, you should decide on some sort of policy. Are you going to take on concessions, or *bursaries* as some therapists call it? If you are, how many? Some therapists have a policy of taking on two bursaries at a time. In other words, they see two clients a week at a knockdown price. Some therapists do this on principle, for political reasons, because they feel that the people who really need therapy the most are the ones who can afford it least. Once you have decided if you will take on bursaries, you should decide how much you can afford to take off your regular price. This will give you some kind of measuring stick when you do get requests for concessions.

You may feel that you want to have your fees on a *sliding scale*. One big therapy organisation, for example, used to charge clients one thousandth of their annual income per session. You need to set the top and bottom points of your sliding scale, and then aim at receiving an hourly rate of about half way between the two. You can check regularly what your average rate is and then make decisions about moving the points, or not taking on any more low cost clients. You may find it tricky where to place an individual client on you scale, however intuition usually works. If in doubt, ask, because clients are unlikely to place themselves at the bottom of your scale.

Objections Unrelated to Money

One solution to this problem, assuming you can offer it and that it is viable to your business, is to offer people who genuinely cannot afford it something cheaper, a different service as it were. It may be that you could offer them a half session at half the price of a full session, or you could see them, instead of once a week, once a fortnight. If they object to this arrangement, (and in nine cases out of ten they will), then the real issue for them is not about price but about value for money. It is their belief that what you offer is not worth what you are charging. In these cases, you need to address the issue of the value of what you do, not the fact that they cannot afford it.

However, before you start turning these objections around into a sale and turning these potential clients into actual clients, get their name and address. After all, they phoned you up, so they must be interested. It's worth putting them on your mailing list so that you can send them some promotional material at various intervals. After all, if their circumstances change, or they change their mind, you will have reminded them through your mailings.

You should be converting at least 50% of enquiries into new clients (if you are gifted at selling over the phone then your rate of conversion should be 70% to 90%). If you aren't turning at least a large proportion of these enquiries into potential clients, you are doing something wrong. You need to look at how you sell over the phone and to study this section on selling very carefully. After all, when someone phones you up it usually means they are mostly sold, so it's really a question of dealing successfully with their objections.

Do some role playing with a friend or colleague. Try selling to them over the phone, then switch roles, get some feedback, and make the necessary improvements to your tactics. Another good idea is to get some feedback on how your answerphone message sounds. Make sure the friends or colleagues that you choose will give you honest feedback. They may not want to hurt your feelings and claim that you sound *cute and assertive* when you actually sound like a cross between Donald Duck and a desperate used car salesman.

How to Sell on the Phone

Effective Use of the Phone

The phone is often the first contact you have with potential clients. It is important to use the phone effectively to promote your business and encourage people to come to you. There are a number of points to consider if you are going to answer calls yourself.

Taking Phone Calls

Remember that every caller may be a potential client. You can answer using your company name or your name, depending on how you want to present yourself. Using a company name gives a professional, authoritative impression. Using your own name is more familiar and friendly. You need to decide which approach is appropriate for you and the clients you are working with.

Let the caller talk and find out what they want. Be polite, attentive and listen patiently and sympathetically. Speak clearly and slowly. You want to give a calm, professional impression. Be ready for any questions. It is a good idea to prepare answers to obvious questions so that you can answer clearly and succinctly without hesitation. Keep a note pad and pen by the phone and take down notes recording your conversation. The notes will serve as a reminder when you've put the phone down. It doesn't look good to phone back to check on something! Keep your records within reach of the phone.

Always take the caller's name, telephone number and address. You can mail them further information that will help encourage them to come to you. The more people who have your leaflet the better. A leaflet will serve as a reminder to a potential client. People may pass it on to others who are interested to.

Separate business line

If you are working from home it is best, though costly, to have a separate business line installed. A separate line can prevent your business from interfering with your domestic life. You know when you answer the business phone that it will be about business. You can answer in a professional way and be prepared. Your family will be protected from nuisance calls and won't have to take endless messages for you. When you've finished work for the day, you can put the answering machine on and avoid being on call around the clock.

If you can afford it, get one, it's definitely worth the initial cost (and remember, a business line is tax deductible).

Distractions

Don't answer the phone during therapy sessions. Your client will feel justly dismayed if they don't have your full attention during the time they have paid for. The person on the phone won't have your full attention either. While an answering machine can be useful for taking

125

messages when you are busy with a client, remember that the noise of the phone ringing, and someone leaving a message is a distraction. Turn the ringing tone of the phone off, and the volume on the answering machine down, if they can be heard in your consulting room.

Answering machines

It's best to try to answer calls yourself. The next best thing is to have someone else to answer the phone when you're not there. If you can't be there to answer calls personally and there's no one else to do it, then an answering machine is indispensable. However, answer machines do put some people off and they won't leave a message.

If they do leave a message, return the call quickly. A caller could be going through a list of therapists in a phone book. If you take too long to call back they will go elsewhere! Get an answering machine that you can call from outside and replay your messages. This way you can return peoples' calls even if you can't get home. Remember that calls are cheaper in the evenings and at weekends. It is also cheaper and quicker to phone than to write.

The message

Leave a short, clear message on your machine. Long-winded messages may put people off. Say who you are, using your company name or your own name, depending on how you've decided to present your business. Apologise for not being able to take the call personally. Ask them to leave their name and number and a good time for you to return their call. You could say what times you will be available to take calls personally, although some people might decide to call you back later, rather than leave a message, and then forget to. Thank people for calling. Check your out-going message occasionally by calling in yourself. They can malfunction sometimes and the distortion is unnerving.

Typical message

A typical message should be something like the following.

Hello. This is 'Massage for Mums'. I'm sorry that there is no one here to answer your call at the moment. Please leave your name, phone number and a convenient time for us to return your call and we will get back to you as soon as possible. Thank you for calling.

Returning calls

Be discreet about returning calls. Make sure you are talking to the right person before saying who you are or what the call is about. Check that they are free to talk to you. They may be in a busy office or within earshot of people who they don't want to overhear the conversation.

Mobile Phones

Mobile phones are useful if you run a mobile business or if you are *on call*. You can always be contacted and always have a phone handy to return calls. Mobile phones have answering machine services so it is easy for you to take your messages and return calls promptly.

A mobile phone may be a more useful, cheaper alternative to having a separate business line installed. However, it is more expensive to phone a mobile phone than to phone a normal phone, and this may put people off.

Freephone Numbers

Freephone numbers, such as 0800 numbers, allow people to call you free of charge, which will certainly encourage callers. However, it is quite expensive; you pay for all the incoming calls plus any extra fees.

Five Golden Rules to Answering the Phone

1. Speak slowly and clearly (even if you are very excited)

Most people tend to speak very quickly when speaking on the phone, especially when they are new to handling telephone enquiries and thus quite uncomfortable with it.

However, keep in mind that speaking slowly and in a relaxed fashion can make all the difference between sounding professional and sounding like an amateur. If you sound calm over the phone, the caller will get the impression that you are also calm when you practise therapy. If you sound rather garbled, hurried or out of breath, then the person may get a rather less favourable mental image of you.

2. Let the Caller Talk

Although the caller is phoning you and is probably expecting you to do most of the explaining, it is important that you do not take over the conversation. Let the caller talk. To this end you must avoid giving any lengthy detail and explanations, especially at the beginning of the call.

An easy way to avoid taking over the conversation is to keep asking the caller questions. Ask them their name and details, ask where they heard about your practice and why they are interested. Find out as much as you can about them. Not only will this put them at ease and give the impression that you are interested in them, it will make selling your services that much easier.

3. Stay on Topic

When you do find yourself giving lengthy explanations of your practice, make sure that what you say is relevant to the question that the caller has asked. Do not, for example give the caller a detailed description of your expertise if they have only asked the question "I'm feeling a bit run down, can homeopathy help increase my energy levels?". It seems obvious, but it's surprising how much a person can bounce from one topic to the next, especially if they are nervous. While it may seem to you that your two minute monologue on your therapy is very interesting and informative, in reality you will probably just end up losing their attention and interest.

4. Use Your Voice

Since the way you use your voice is almost the only way that the caller can create an image of you over the phone, use it to advantage. Listen to yourself when you are speaking: if you sound enthusiastic and energetic about what you are saying, the caller will get the impression that you are both of these things. If you sound very monotone and bored, then the caller will probably have absolutely no desire to meet you in person.

If you are not sure how you sound on the phone, record a couple of conversations with a tape recorder. You will probably be amazed at the difference between how you think you sounded and how you actually do sound. Remember, it's not so much what you say as how you say it.

5. Talk Sense and Be Positive

Try to use positive language whenever you can. Admittedly this is not possible all the time but, with practice, you will find that negative terms can almost always be replaced with positive ones.

It is also a good habit to avoid using the specialised language of your practice. This is particularly important for psychotherapists and counsellors. Make the safe, if not entirely correct, assumption that none of the people who call know what *object relations* or *feedback* are. Explain things in simple and accessible language and you will making the caller feel excluded from your *world*.

Once again, it will be very useful for you to listen to yourself speaking on the phone and make a note of the phrases that you find yourself repeating. Are they negative or positive? Is there a better way of putting something that you have said? It is worth sitting down and taking the time to really find out how you sound on the phone, after all, your first contact with almost all of your clients will be over the phone.

How Not to Handle a Phone Enquiry

Let's start this chapter with an example of how not to deal with a telephone enquiry:

For the sake of an example, let's assume that someone is phoning the number of an aromatherapist whose advert they have recently seen in an issue of *Holistic London Guide.*

Someone answers: "Hello".

Caller: "Is this the Aromatherapy Centre?"

Therapist: "Yes it is".

Caller: "Do you have practitioners there, can I come and get an aromatherapy massage?"

Therapist: "Yes you can".

Caller: "Thanks, I'll make a note of that and I'll give you a ring later to make an appointment"

Therapist: "Alright, thanks for calling". Both hang up.

All in all that was a very short, uninformative and slightly dissatisfying exchange for both parties, agreed? Let's look at why. First of all, answering the phone. When you answer the phone it is a good idea, if not essential for projecting a professional image, that you state your own name or that of your business. It's a very simple thing to do but surprisingly, many people who work out of their own home don't bother.

The second thing missing from this exchange is that the therapist didn't ask for the caller's details. It's a good idea to get the name, number and address of every person who rings with an enquiry, this way you can build up your mailing list and perhaps follow up on the enquiry by mailing the person a leaflet or brochure. Remember, once they hang up you have no way of knowing who they were or of contacting them again - even if they sounded really interested in your service, they may forget, or give up on the idea of aromatherapy.

If you don't get the all-important details, then you are losing out on a very easy sales opportunity. Obviously they have heard about you from somewhere and are already partially sold on your service, since they bothered to give you a call in the first place; take advantage of this opportunity by giving them every reason in the world to become your client.

On that note, a very useful thing to find out from callers is how they heard about your business; perhaps they are responding to a recommendation from an existing client, or have seen your promotional material in a local health food store, maybe they saw one of your ads in a magazine, in this case, which magazine was it? This is an essential way of monitoring the effectiveness of your promotional material and your ads. You may even find that you have other marketing outlets that you didn't know about, such as a really good reputation in the local arts school. You never know!

It is also vital that you make the caller feel good. In the example above, the therapist thanked the client for calling. That's a good start, but perhaps they could have also offered to send the caller some more information or offer to book an appointment over the phone. The worst impression you can give over the phone is that the caller is somehow inconveniencing you, in fact, this a very useful method of getting rid of unwanted callers!

Next, find out what that person wants *now*! Why are they calling, what do they need, what do they want from your therapy. In the example above, the therapist could have asked if the caller had one particular problem that aromatherapy massage could help with, or if they just wanted to relax. The therapist could also have asked whether the caller had ever had aromatherapy treatment before. It's important to keep in mind that this person is calling for a reason: find out what it is! Don't be shy, practise getting as much information from the caller as is appropriate. The more information you get, the more you will know what that particular person's needs are and the easier it will be to sell them on your therapy. Once you know what they need, all you have to do is tell them how you are going to fulfil those needs (within reason).

Finally, suggest to the caller a course of action. You could tell them the times you are available for a session that week and offer to book them in. You might ask them what times are convenient for them, and suggest which of those you are available for. You could suggest that they come in soon for a information session, or a consultation. It is understandable that you don't want to sound pushy, but remember that *they* called *you* up, and probably with the idea that they wanted to book an appointment or find out more information. Well, the best way to get more information is to come in and speak to you face to face. Make it easy for them and they will come.

Handling Phone Enquiries The Easy Way

The most vital aspect of answering the phone has nothing to do with actually answering the phone, but is this: keep a pad of paper and a pen next to the phone at all times! This might sound rather obvious, but many therapists are actually quite disorganised when it comes to these smaller, more trivial details. To be honest, who hasn't asked a caller to hold the line while they look for their appointment book, a pen or paper or all three in succession? Although this is a just small detail and shouldn't reflect upon you as a therapist, it does nothing to inspire the confidence of the caller.

So, keep the area around the phone tidy. Keep your appointment book, a large blank book for messages and several pens next to the phone. If you have to, there is nothing wrong with chaining a pen to the phone or to the wall.

In your message book (or on the cover) have a list of key information that you want to get from each caller and perhaps a list of responses to important questions from them. For example, in the list of key information you should put 'caller name, number and address' and 'where caller heard about us'. In your list of responses you might have a well-written little phrase to describe your particular therapy and also your address, telephone number, postal code etc. Use this more as a prompting device for yourself, rather than as a set script. Be natural on the phone, be yourself, not a script.

When Someone Else is Answering Your Phone

If it is not possible for you to answer the phone yourself and you have someone else do it for you, make sure that they are properly trained.

Callers will often judge your business by the way their enquiry is dealt with; this is not always a conscious thing, but in this day and age of endless choice, it is an easy and natural way of easing the decision-making process.

Make sure that every person who answers your phone is well versed in handling enquiries and that they are fed the proper information by you. They must know exactly what it is that you do, the location of your practice and also some idea of how to give directions to it, the times that you are available during the day to see clients, the price of your service, and when you will be available to speak to the caller personally, if that is what they prefer.

Spend some time training them. Engage in some role-playing and make sure that you cover every angle of your business. Anyone who handles enquiries should be confident and able to answer any questions about your business.

Be Positive

If you are a counsellor or psychotherapist, you are probably trained to use language that is very transparent, that isn't pushy or influencing. However, this kind of language is not exactly positive either. For example, you probably use phrases such as "I don't know", "perhaps", "it may well be", "I'm not sure". As a counsellor, you are often dealing with very difficult issues and don't want to barge in and influence your client's processes too much.

While this is very good in counselling, it is inappropriate when it comes to selling and getting your clients to come initially. Remember when you make the initial contact that you are a salesperson, not a counsellor (you are only a counsellor when you are being paid to be one). When someone asks if your therapy can help with their depression, don't say, "Well it could do, but it is important not to set yourself up for disappointment or failure" or "I don't know, there is no guarantee". These are very negative responses and are to be avoided.

Being positive doesn't mean that you have to lie. It's imperative that you tell the truth, but you can phrase the truth in a very positive light. Here is a sample dialogue.

A client phones up in a state of depression and wants to know: "Will psychotherapy cure depression?"

You could respond by saying: "The only real long term solution to depression is psychotherapy. There are many short-term cures for depression such as exercise, eating a healthier diet, all of these things will help you to some extent, but these solutions do not get to the heart of the issue. Depression is a very complex phenomena, it is made up of many interconnected issues. The way I work is to work on one issue at a time, and focus thoroughly on each of these issue. This is a very effective way of working because it means that we can resolve each of these particular issues so that you start to feel better early on in the therapy and you realise that there is an end to it. This will increase your confidence in working on each successive issue as it is uncovered."

Alternatively, you could say: "Well, there are no guarantees. It may work for you and the thing with psychotherapy is that it can be hit and miss. I don't know. Generally it does work with people but it is hard going."

Now both of these responses are 'true', but the first one expresses your belief in what you are doing, while the second one is very negative. Which response would be more convincing to you? Remember if you are going to do therapy and you are going to go once a week at £30 a session, £1500 a year, £3000 over two years. Are you going to pay out £3000 for something that has been described to you as possibly failing?. You need to be *positive*, and also *honest*, to help them feel good about coming to your therapy in the first place. The client has to be made to feel, indeed they want to feel, that they are making the right choice.

What are the differences between the two responses? The second response focuses on the fact that there is no guarantee that your therapy will cure depression. Well, this is true, you can never be sure that therapy will cure depression, but why focus on this? Don't make one of the weaknesses of psychotherapy the highlight of your conversation. The second response doesn't really explain what your therapy is, why the caller should seriously consider embarking on your therapy, so it doesn't really have the depth of the first response, it's rather vague.

The first explanation is sharper, more confident, and a more intelligent response. It explains why your therapy is so effective for treating depression, how your therapy works, that therapy is a process that happens in stages and that there will be noticeable results in a short time, which seems to be the client's primary concern. The first explanation really addresses the concerns of the clients whereas the second doesn't.

It is good to be positive on the phone, but it is also very useful to be firm with enquiries when you don't feel that you can help. For example, if the caller says, "I've got a bad ankle, will acupuncture be useful in treating this?" Your response might be "I've never treated anyone with an ankle injury. I don't think it will work".

This is a firm and positive response. Don't worry that you have lost a potential client; after all, if you really cannot help them and they end up trying your therapy unsuccessfully, you will have an irate client on your hands.

On the other hand if you give your true opinion, the caller will probably be quite pleased to find someone who is honest and tells them exactly what they think. You can still get their details and mail to them, perhaps they will need acupuncture at a later date. You may also find that it is not the end of the conversation. They may be interested in the other benefits of acupuncture. Perhaps they also suffer from fatigue, in this case you can explain to them the benefits of your therapy in helping with general tiredness and feelings of being rundown. You've got yourself a customer! You may also be able to pass them on to a colleague in another discipline with whom you have a reciprocal agreement to refer clients.

So don't give up if you feel that you really cannot address the concerns of a potential client, even if you can only explain to them what the benefits of your therapy are and get them on your mailing list, it hasn't been a waste of time. Above all, if you are going to get the most out of telephone enquiries, you should learn to become fluent and comfortable on the phone and learn to enjoy telling people about the benefits of what you do. This will increase your confidence and success rate when it comes to selling.

Building a Referral Network

Developing 'Influencers'

Influencers are people who will influence other people to buy your services. They may be past clients, present clients, colleagues, training organisations, citizens advice bureaux, other practitioners and other people and organisations you may only be dimly aware of. They are the people that your potential clients are likely to ask if they are looking for a therapist.

Influencers are valuable because of the amount of independence and authority they carry when recommending someone. Independence in the sense of not having a vested interest when they do refer to a particular practitioner, and authority because they may have some knowledge (or perceived knowledge) about choice of therapist. Influencers are worth cultivating because of this value and because they will repeat their message to other potential clients and will continue to be a constant source of clients.

To get an idea of who your influencers might be, imagine a member of the public trying to find someone who practises osteopathy, for example. Who might they ask? It might be a friend or partner. It might be a friend of a friend. The question might be phrased; 'I'm looking for an osteopath, do you know one you would recommend? If they draw a blank with this they might ask acquaintances where they should look to find one. They might ask their GP, social worker or local health food shop owner. They might look in the Yellow Pages of the phone book for an osteopath (this therapy is listed as a separate category, but many therapies do not have their own listing). They might pay a visit to their local library (or phone them) to try to find a list of osteopaths. They might phone up an acupuncturist from the Yellow Pages and ask them if they know of an osteopath in the area.

How they go about the process of finding a therapist will depend on many factors. They may have many friends who are already interested in the holistic field who they will look to as a source of information. Conversely they may have few friends in the field and will look elsewhere for a recommendation.

It's worthwhile to think about the different ways in which a member of the public would go about finding a therapist and to make a list of them. This is a useful exercise, one of putting yourself in your potential clients' boots, because it focuses on who *out there* might be your ally in referring clients to you. Reading the rest of this section will also give you some ideas of who they might be.

Once you have made a list, the next vital steps are to:

1. Make yourself known to the people on this list. It's worthwhile speaking to someone in particular, either over the phone, or better still face to face. People are more likely to refer to you if they have met you and feel they can trust you. The last thing they want to do is to refer members of the public to a therapist they do not trust. And trust if built from experience in dealing with you.

2. Tell them you are available to see clients, and would be pleased if they would refer clients to you. It's not enough to make contact and let them know what you do, you also need to make it clear that you are looking for clients and how happy you would be if they could pass people on to you.

3. Leave them with enough information to make it easy for them to refer to you. Make sure they have got your details and if they are willing, your business card or brochure. A number of brochures or leaflets might be advisable if they are likely to give them out to members of the public. If you move address don't forget to let them know of the changes.

Past and Present Clients

The people likely to be most vocal about you are your former and present clients. Present clients will have you on their mind much of the time if they are seeing you on a regular basis. They may be telling their friends they are having sessions with you. Hopefully, they will be singing your praises and trying to persuade their friends to see you as

136

well especially if they know you have spaces for more clients. However it's not all rosy. Your present clients may not want their friends in therapy with you: they may want you all for themselves; they may worry they will be discussed by you and their friend; they may worry about information being disclosed that they do not wish disclosed. In this case, you may need to find a tactful opportunity to reassure them of the confidentiality of the sessions.

In counselling, it is more of a problem if you have two clients who are friends. Obviously you will maintain confidentiality, but unforeseen complications can occur. Your clients may meet each other on the doorstep. They may talk about you and exchange information with each other which may be difficult if you are a counsellor who believes in remaining *opaque* because of transference issues. They may talk about their friends in therapy and give different versions of events, which may complicate issues.

Past clients are also good referral sources. Whilst they may not be proselytising as much as your present clients, if their friends ask them if they know of a therapist, they will recommend you. Past clients do not have the same complications as present clients. The longer you have been practising, the more past clients you will accumulate and the more you will come to rely on them for referrals. Don't forget to keep them informed if you change address. It's more of a problem if they move address and you lose contact with them. To avoid this, when you mail them a leaflet, include an accompanying letter, which not only confirms contact, but in which you ask them to inform you if they move address.

Colleagues and Fellow Practitioners

You probably already have a network of people that you trained with. Or you may have made contact with other practitioners in your area for either mutual support or friendship, having your practices in common. It may be that you already cross refer to each other. If not, why not?

If you wish to increase the number of fellow practitioners you have, then some networking is in order. The question is how do you approach other practitioners? The most appropriate way would be to contact them directly and ask them if they mind you referring potential clients to them. It's likely they will say 'no' and you will have immediately made a friend. They may offer to return the favour, which you should graciously accept. Don't worry too much if they don't. They probably will in time.

Having colleagues in a similar profession to yours can be mutually supportive and lead to friendship. Being a sole practitioner can be a lonely business and having someone to talk with about your work can bring you both together. It may be that the trust is such that you consider going into business together. There can be mutual cost benefits such as sharing printing costs and room hire, but more importantly the idea of doing something new together can be exhilarating. Like marriage, you can celebrate wedding anniversaries, or end up experiencing the bitter pains of divorce.

Training Centres

Training centres do much to market themselves and a large part of their budget is spent on marketing and promotion. The public will often look to training organisations for a therapist in the belief that the therapists they recommend must be fully trained and qualified. They imagine that these are a safer bet than finding a practitioner through an advertising or listing in a classified directory. Thus they convey much authority when referring.

Many of the training institutes have a policy of passing on enquiries to therapists who work on their faculty or who have trained with them. If you are considering training with an organisation, it's worth asking the management if they have a referral service you can depend on for clients when you have finished the training. Will they automatically refer them to you? Is there a priority attached to their referrals (there is often an unofficial policy of referring)? How many clients a year are they likely to pass on to you? What is their geographic catchment area? (This is important if you wish to move out of town at a later stage).

If you have finished training then you may already be getting clients from them. If this is so, it's best to keep in regular contact. Either phone or (better still) meet face to face with the faculty and administration. You might consider doing further postgraduate training with the organisation that trained you if appropriate, not only to improve your effectiveness as a therapist, but to make contact with the faculty and other colleagues who may also be useful referral sources.

If you are not getting clients from your training centre, it's worth contacting them and asking them why not. It might simply be that they have lost contact with you, or you've disappeared from their minds. It may be that they get few enquiries from the public and therefore do not offer this service. Much of their promotion goes into finding new trainees and not members of the public, so their enquiries from the public may be few and far between.

Community And Government Organisations

If you have heavily promoted yourself in your surrounding area you will probably receive calls from organisations who want to know more about what you do. They may come from various departments of social services who get requests from their 'cases' for treatments; GPs; Citizens Advice Bureau; state bodies serving special needs; drug dependency clinics etc.

The individuals at these organisations need to know that you are *risk free*, that you are not part of some *loony sect*, *a rip off merchant*, *untrained* or *unqualified*. Their job may be on the line if they refer one of their 'cases' to you and that person claims the therapy has been a waste of time, or worse still, has damaged them. You will need to reassure these people that you are a *bone fide* therapist, are fully trained, fully qualified, a member of a recognised professional body and have been practising for years. If things go wrong they can always explain to their supervisor that they did their best to verify your credentials and it is therefore not their fault. So if you get a call from a member of one of these organisations and they want to know more about you, don't just send them a brochure, talk with them further on the phone. Reassure that person and tell him/her just how qualified you are. Convince him or her that you are a respectable citizen. Be willing to visit them and talk with them about their clients and how you can be of service.

Once one of these organisations begin referring clients to you, you should broadcast this fact to other similar organisations. If you tell them you currently get referrals from your GP, you immediately become *official* in their eyes and they will feel much more comfortable about referring clients to you.

If the sessions go well with the clients they refer to you, those clients are likely to report back and you will find more clients coming your way.

If you have not been contacted by any official bodies, consider approaching them directly. It's easy enough to get a list of GP's from the *Yellow Pages*. You can mail doctors directly with a leaflet. It is best if the leaflet that you use is in *officialspeak* and uses terms that doctors are familiar with. Saying you spent two years in Mexico experimenting with peyote to reach higher stages of consciousness may look good on a leaflet aimed at the middle classes in Camden, however doctors are more conservative and are likely to toss your leaflet into the bin. Do include a short covering letter, which should give your credentials.

There are many organisations, statutory and voluntary, which can become sources of referrals for you. To find a list of them, a trip to your local library is the best option. Some councils publish directories of services that are on offer to residents. The title of the directory may be something like 'A Directory of Community Organisations in Merton'. Depending on your type of therapy you will need to decide which bodies are best to contact. The majority of organisations listed will not be of much use to you, but you should be able to find several you can use. It's best to phone up to get a name and send your leaflet and letter to them personally. Then follow up with a further telephone call.

Retailers

Some retail outlets that may refer the public to practitioners are: holistic health centres, health food shops, essential oil shops, New Age Shops, book shops specialising in holistic subjects, wholefood cafes and some chemists with a holistic slant. If a retail outlet has a notice board for the public to read which carries business cards and flyers of practitioners, or if they have a rack full of such brochures, then this is the one you should focus your attention on. Such a retail outlet has permitted itself to be an information provider and the public feel more at ease asking the staff for further information. A customer might pick up a particular flyer and ask one of the staff 'Do you know anything about this type of meditation?' At which point, if it was your flyer, you would wish the staff person to say 'Yes, I hear it's very powerful and

I've heard lots of good things about it' followed by further favourable comments.

So how should you approach these outlets? Bear in mind they are in business and want to be financially successful. So favours should be two way. Here are some ideas:

1. Take a part-time job there. That way you will get to know the staff personally and they can all become your personal PR assistants.
2. Offer to recommend the shop to your clients in exchange for referrals.
3. Tell them that you regularly tour the area dropping off your leaflets and you can drop off their leaflets and put up their posters in exchange for referrals.
4. Offer to include their brochure in your mailouts in exchange for...
5. Offer them therapy sessions in exchange for...
6. Ask the staff directly. Tell them you're a practitioner and ask them to send any interested customers to you.
7. Visit the retail outlet often and become a regular customer, the staff will get to know more about you and what you do.
8. If they have a spare room, suggest you offer your therapy on the premises. They will make some money from room rental and it may attract extra customers.

Networking is something you may either love or hate. Some practitioners thrive on meeting others with business in mind, in either formal or informal settings. Other practitioners hate the whole idea and would prefer to write copy and design adverts.

You can use whatever avenue suits your personality, and you feel most comfortable doing. Sometimes you may find that you have to develop skills in areas which feel like more of a challenge to you.

A Checklist For Getting More Clients

All of the following have been covered in detail elsewhere in this book, but they are collected here so that you can quickly run through them. The list is not in any particular order of preference.

1. Apply to the local GPs in your area to see whether they have a practice for alternative practitioners. You can get a list from the Yellow Pages or the local library.

2. Put a card up on your local notice boards. Make sure it looks professional. There is nothing worse than a tatty looking card. To find notice boards in your area you can just drive or walk around looking for them in likely places such as wholefood cafes and shops, libraries, newsagents etc.

3. Tell as many people as you can that you are in business and what you do. You can pick up clients wherever you go by publicising yourself.

4. Tell other practitioners in your locality what you do. Arrange to meet and talk with them. If they practise a different therapy from you, you can refer clients on to each other.

   For example if you're an acupuncturist and someone goes to your aromatherapist contact and asks about acupuncture, they can refer the client to you. If they practise the same therapy as you, they may be willing to refer clients on to you if they are full, or if you live in a different part of town.

5. Get yourself listed in as many directories as possible. There are many directories around that list practitioners. Some are more specialised than others and may just list practitioners who practise what you do. Some are more general. You may be well aware of them anyway. If the listings are free it's certainly a good idea to get your name in them.

6. Get yourself registered at any institutes or centres that hold lists of practitioners such as the *Institute of Complementary Medicine* who will refer clients on to you if you register with them.

7. Approach your local holistic health centres and see if they have space for practitioners. They may also have a notice board where you can pin up a notice or somewhere you can display your leaflet.

8. Get leaflets printed about what you do and distribute them locally.

9. Get a business card printed and give it to everyone you meet. They can be very useful for the impromptu meeting or visit.

10. Consider opening up a holistic health centre. This does require capital and lots of thought but it's sometimes easier to get it together with a group of other practitioners.

11. Promote yourself on the radio and television (see relevant sections in this book).

12. Give a talk or demonstration on the type of therapy you do.

13. Consider writing a book. When you are an author, people view you as an authority on the subject. This adds to your status and is an aid in getting clients.

14. You could also consider producing a video if your therapy lends itself to the medium of the VDU. Some subjects do, others don't. Body therapies such as massage, reflexology, shiatsu and Tai Chi transfer well to video.

15. Produce an audio tape. This is relatively easy to do and does not require a great deal of capital. Again, certain therapies, like hypnotherapy and meditation lend themselves to this.

16. You could hold a workshop. They are a way of meeting a larger number of people. They will attract a different type of client as people who enjoy workshops will enjoy being part of a group. It may be that these clients will then enter into therapy with you on a one-to-one basis.

17. You could join an *existing* network or consider setting up a network with other practitioners to jointly put together leaflets and share advertising costs. You will also be able to refer clients between yourselves.

18. Take a stand at festivals to meet both other practitioners and the public. You could give out your leaflets and tell them about what you do and possibly offer 'taster' treatments.

19. Write an article about yourself and get it published in your local paper.

20. Maintain contact with the therapy organisation you trained with. They may refer clients on to you. This depends on their policy. It may be that you have to be actively involved with this training organisation before they'll do this. But there is no harm in making and maintaining contact with them.

21. Think of running specialist courses aimed at specialist groups. For example, you could target GPs in your area and run a stress related workshop especially for GPs. This has the added benefit of connecting you with your GPs so that they may refer patients to you.

22. Produce a leaflet and distribute it widely.

23. You could exchange your client list with another practitioner. You mail to their clients and they mail to yours.

24. You can tell your existing clients that you have spaces available and they may well find new clients for you or have someone in mind. Certainly clients you have presently and have had in the past will be more than willing to refer their friends to you if your relationship with them was okay.

Having said that there are certain exceptions to this, for instance if you are a counsellor, clients may not want their friends to know about you because they worry about confidentiality.

25. Think about targeting companies rather than individuals. Companies are becoming more and more conscious of how therapy can assist them and make their employees more productive. There is a lot in the media about stress-related causes of absenteeism.

26. Mail your leaflet or information about any workshops you may be doing to past clients. They may pass your leaflet on to other people and recommend them to you. There is nothing like a personal recommendation from former clients.

27. There may be shops in your area that are willing to refer clients to you. For instance shops selling aromatherapy oils might refer interested customers to you, if you are on good terms with them. You may even consider working in the shop on a part-time basis.

28. Teach your therapy at an adult education institute. Your new students will advertise on your behalf. It also adds some authority to what you do to say that you teach the subject.

29. Make sure you are listed in the *Yellow Pages* and *Thompsons* under your particular therapy (if they have a listing for that therapy). *Thompsons* will list you free, and *Yellow Pages* will give you a free listing if you have a business line.

30. Any event that you put on could appear in a pre-listing section of your local newspaper or magazine. You may be aware of the free listings, so it is simply a matter of ringing them or sending them a flier through the post about it.

31. If you are in supervision, mention to your supervisor that you need clients. He or she may have an abundance of clients and refer the overspill to you.

32. Join any groups of similar practitioners in the area who have formed an association.

33. Talk with other similar practitioners and ask them how they get their clients. Exchanging information in this way is beneficial to all and you may learn things that you hadn't thought of. You can also learn from their mistakes. *It is much better to learn from other people's mistakes than from your own.*

34. If you are or have been involved with any religious organisation, they may be happy to refer clients to you.

35. If you are experienced enough, you could set up a training in your therapy. At the end of the day, your trainees may become referral sources for you.

36. Try to maintain a referral network of colleagues practising the same therapy. Cross referring people between yourselves can be very profitable. This is likely to happen particularly if the other practitioners live in a different area from you. They will refer clients who live in your area to you. Otherwise these clients will be a wasted opportunity.

37. Think about doing further training with an organisation that has a good referral service. When you have finished the training, you will automatically have a client base.

Computers

Do You Need a Computer?

If you are a sole practitioner you can live without a computer. A simple set of index cards purchased from a stationery shop will suffice. Even an appointment book with an address section is sufficient and more convenient than a computer, as you can keep it by the phone or carry it with you. However a computer can be used for all sorts of business purposes, such as mail shots, producing your leaflet on screen, keeping notes on clients, writing a book and a host of other uses.

The main drawback of using a computer is your time. Your time is precious. Every hour you spend trying to learn a new programme or fix a bug could be spent seeing a client. So think carefully before investing in a computer. Remember to cost for your time spent at the computer, as this will far outweigh the cost of the computer itself.

If you have a computer and are familiar with the use of the database, try to use this as your message book. Place the phone next to the computer and type in the information as the caller tells you. If you find this a little too distracting, then enter the information in your database after you have spoken to the caller, making sure that you include the date of the enquiry in the entry. This is an easy way to update your database and will save you a lot of work in the future when it comes to printing mailing lists and invoices, etc. However using a database is not crucial and you could keep your records on a word processor.

If you are not computer literate it might be worth becoming so and buying yourself a computer. You may find it hard to financially justify for your business, however, because its can be hard to estimate how much worth it will be to you until you have learnt how to use it. If you've got the time and money and want one, then buy one. Take a short computer course, or buy a book on computers, such as one of the books in the *Computers for Dummies* series. Investing in and learning how to use a computer can make your life much easier. At the very least you will learn patience.

The Internet

The internet is not likely to be of much use to the holistic therapist for self promotion. First of all, it's expensive. You will need to buy a computer, if you have not already bought one, a modem, and pay a fee to be hooked up to an 'internet provider'. All of this costs a considerable amount of money. If you want to be 'found' by an internet browser, you will need to have a 'web site' which costs several hundred pounds to set up, and more money to maintain. This is assuming you know the technicalities of the system, if not then add the price of paying someone to design and create a web site for you. Add to these the costs of phone charges, software and peripherals. For the small number of clients you are likely to capture (if any), you will find it's not a worthwhile proposition.

A cheaper approach is to email people or groups who might be interested (similar to mailing letters in bulk, but which is much less expensive than the postal system). However, 'junk mail' abounds on the system and you could find yourself being locked out if you simply mail all and sundry with details of your workshops.

Secondly, internet users are not your target audience. While the total number of users worldwide is huge, few are likely to live or work close to you. Furthermore, half the users on the internet are male, under thirty years of age and into computers. Not exactly your holistic types, so leave the internet to the nerds.

Finally, if you've used the internet you will know that it takes a lot of time to find something useful out there to hook into. The same goes for someone trying to find you. Two needles trying to find each other in a haystack. For some, it's exciting, but for me the information super highway is about as exciting as visiting a local library.

For certain practitioners the internet may have its uses. Celebrity workshop leaders can perhaps use the Internet, either for emailing journalists and publications about their impending activities. If they travel overseas giving talks, they can use email as it's better than phoning or faxing, being quicker and cheaper. For most practitioners, though, it's not a worthwhile proposition.

Index